I Stole Freddie Mercur

MALCOLM HARDEE is a stand-up comic, promoter and runs Up The Creek in Greenwich. This is his first autobiography.

'It has been an honour and a pleasure to know Malcolm Hardee over the past years. I am thrilled that he has included me in his memoirs and sincerely hope and expect ninety-nine per cent of what he has written to be bare-faced lies.' – JOOLS HOLLAND

'A hilarious, anarchic living legend; a millennial Falstaff. This book is just like being with Malcolm only you don't have to hire a solicitor afterwards.' – ROB NEWMAN

'South London's king of comedy, Malcolm Hardee is a natural clown who in any decent country would be a national institution.' – STEWART LEE, *Vox*

'Malcolm Hardee took his clothes off – a spectacle about as funny as being electrocuted . . . He looks like Eric Morecambe's kid brother and is famed for appearing buck naked with only a few inflated balloons to protect the nation from the spectral horror of his private parts. In macho Edinburgh he decided to dispense with the props and never in my life – not since I was three years old, anyway – have I so yearned to see a balloon.' – JAN MOIR, *OBSERVER*

'Malcolm Hardee, the South London Rabelais, has led his life as though for the perfect autobiography and now he has paid himself the compliment of writing it. (Will this do, Malcolm?)' – ARTHUR SMITH

I STOLE
FREDDIE MERCURY'S
BIRTHDAY CAKE

MALCOLM HARDEE
with JOHN FLEMING

FOURTH ESTATE · London

First published in Great Britain in 1996 by
Fourth Estate Limited
6 Salem Road
London, W2 4BU

Copyright © 1996 by Malcolm Hardee and John Fleming

A catalogue record for this book is available
from the British Library

ISBN 1–85702–385–4

Typeset by Rowland Phototypesetting Ltd,
Bury St Edmunds, Suffolk
Printed in Great Britain by
Clays Ltd, St Ives plc

CONTENTS

LIST OF PHOTOGRAPHS

Unless otherwise credited the copyright in all pictures is held by Malcolm Hardee or his mum.

Chapter 1

Near Someone Famous

It is 1996, I am forty-six years old and I have all my own teeth.

This story starts on 5 January (the day before Epiphany) 1950, when I was born, the first son of Frank and Joan Hardee, in the Tuberculosis Ward of Lewisham Hospital in South East London. Immediately after my birth, I was taken from my mother and moved to an orphanage in a place aptly named Ware in Hertfordshire. My mother had tuberculosis, and, in those days, it was unknown for working-class fathers to look after young children. We were not to meet again for nearly two years.

My dad was a lighterman, as were his father and his father before him. He worked on the River Thames, pulling lighters – barges – with his tugboat or, in the early days, with ponies. Physically he was a cross between Frankie Howerd and Denis Healey, a solid, well-built man, and his nickname among the riverfolk was Tiddler.

His first parental act came when I was one day old and he bought me a train set, which of course I didn't see for those first couple of years. It was a steam train fuelled by methylated spirits, held in a little container underneath the engine, and it ran round a big circular track. You lit the methylated spirits which started the piston. Dad set it up in the hall. When I first saw the train, he wouldn't let me play with it. You know what dads are like – he had to set it off. It went so fast it came off the rails and the burning meths set fire to the carpet. Nearly burnt the whole house down.

A lot of people have said I came off the rails myself later on and my mother wonders if this incident accounts for my early interest in pyrotechnics.

When mum was released from the solitary confinement of the TB sanatarium, she came to collect me from the orphanage. She says she nearly chose the wrong child as there was an angelic lookalike sitting contentedly in one corner, quiet as a mouse, and a screaming brat in the other. She moved towards the angel but was ushered away with the brat.

Home was in Lewisham – a mile south of the River Thames at Deptford – at 20 Grover Court, in a modest block of genteel 1930s apartments with flat roofs. They are still there, set back from the main road: two storeys, four apartments to each storey, about a hundred in all. They look a little like holiday flats in some seaside town like Herne Bay or Lyme Regis.

I have almost always lived near someone famous. In Grover Court, I grew up next door to the singer Val Doonican. When we moved from there to another part of Lewisham, Michael Leggo lived next door; he became a TV producer and invented Mr Blobby with Noël Edmonds. After that, I had a flat in Lee Green and three doors up was Mark Knopfler from Dire Straits, though I never talked to him. Later there was musician and TV presenter Jools Holland: he lived over the road from me in Blackheath and we became friends. Now I live about five doors away from Miss Whiplash.

When I was ten or eleven Val Doonican (nice man, poxy initials) taught me to play the mouth organ. It is a skill that has stood me in good stead over the years. He lived with his mum – he must have been in his mid-twenties and wasn't famous then – and used to sit in an old armchair on his porch, playing the guitar. Val came here from Waterford in Ireland with a group called the Four Ramblers, three of whom lived in Grover Court – Val, Pat Campbell and Pat Sherlock. Pat Sherlock's son, Barry, was a couple of years younger than me and my best mate. Pat produced a Sunday afternoon TV show called *The Showbiz XI*, based on football teams. They had the TV All Stars on one side and the Showbiz Eleven on the other – the Showbiz Eleven consisted of people you didn't normally get on telly, like the comedian Norman Wisdom – and members of these teams sometimes came round to Pat's place. I often saw people like pop star Tommy Steele but I

3

was more impressed with Rinty Monahan, the boxing champion. He was the Barry McGuigan of the 1950s and used to sing 'When Irish Eyes Are Smiling' every time he won a fight. He used to muck around with us kids and pretend he was going to hit us. It seemed glamorous.

Pat Campbell went on to be a Radio Luxembourg disc jockey. At around the same time, he assumed a false American accent and recorded 'The Deal' which often pops up as 'one of the worst records ever made'. And it is. It's about a husband who makes a deal with God to take him rather than his dying pregnant wife.

My two grandmothers were highly influential on my upbringing. But they were poles apart. My father's mother, Nanny Hardee, was eccentric, vain and, in appearance, not unlike a young Margaret Rutherford. She was full of airs and graces and often dragged me 'up town' to sit in the Café Royal in Regent Street and watch the real rich people. She was also preoccupied with death and I remember being taken as a treat to a funeral parlour to see my aunt Grace in her coffin. She loved a good funeral, did Nanny Hardee, and it was a big day for her when she was able to tell my mother that she had agreed with funeral directors that mum could go in the Hardee family burial plot – as long as she was cremated first to save space. It was Nanny Hardee's idea of the best possible news she could impart. Grandad Hardee had died at the tender age of thirty-four, but not before he'd given Nanny two sons. He loved riding motorbikes and was a bit of a womaniser. One night when he was coming back from a rendezvous with another woman his bike broke down. It was freezing cold, and he caught pneumonia, which proved fatal. On his deathbed, he made Nanny promise that she'd always be faithful to him – a bit of a cheek, really. But she did and she was.

She had a hard life: one son, Malcolm, was killed at Dunkirk and my father died before her, too, so she outlived all the important men in her life. I'm sure she lavished her unfulfilled love for her husband on my father, Frank, and, in a smaller way, on me.

My other grandmother, Nanny Maude, was the exact opposite to the airs-and-graces aspirations of Nanny Hardee. She was a slight woman who had been in service when she was younger, as a maid. Down-to-earth, she loved a Guinness and, in the 1950s, enjoyed the new fad of bingo. She used to take me to Ramsgate rather than the Café Royal.

Of growing up in the 1950s in South East London, I remember foggy winters and very hot summers. The buildings were dirtier then. All that's gone now and, in a way, it's a shame. We had proper fog in those days – real stuff that made you choke – because everyone had coal fires belching out smoke in the autumn and winter, and they hadn't passed the smoke law. The fogs were a sort of brown–green colour and were known as pea-soupers. To this day, I've never liked pea soup.

The big event of my childhood that sticks out in my mind occurred in November 1957, when I was seven. It happened behind my house. 'The Great Lewisham Train Crash', they called it in the papers. At Lewisham several railway lines cross on two levels, three at the bottom and one over the top. In the November fog, two trains collided on the bottom line in the middle. They shot up in the air and knocked an entire train off the top: 117 people died. My dad's garage was next to the line and afterwards there were carriage wheels lying in it. A brick wall at the back had to be rebuilt after it was hit by a fire engine coming to rescue people.

My aunt Rosemary was at Grover Court that night with her husband, Uncle Doug. He should have travelled on the train that crashed. They heard about it on the radio and I think that was the first time I saw a person in shock.

I didn't hear the crash – it happened at night and I was asleep – but I was made to stay in the house afterwards. A Mrs Fantos, I think, was the heroine of the crash: she went out to the main road and commandeered cars and blankets and stuff. The injured were brought into our car park, probably suffering from post-traumatic shock syndrome although, of course, they didn't have that in those days.

Next morning was when the showbiz bug bit me. I climbed on to the flat roof of our building from where I could see the TV cameras filming the aftermath of the accident. There I was up on the roof waving while they were carting dead bodies about. It was really exciting: our flats were suddenly the centre of almost world-wide attention.

London was different then. There were empty spaces all over the place where German bombs had exploded during the Second World War. We used to play on bomb sites and in air-raid shelters. Some people still had Anderson shelters in their gardens. They had made these themselves by digging a hole in the ground and putting corrugated iron round it; they looked a bit like small Nissen huts. I found old gas masks to play with too.

It was still rather bleak so soon after the war but rationing never affected us much because my dad worked on the river and people who worked on the river tended to get more than other people. They used to have to deal with all the cargo coming in, so we got bananas and things. Perfectly legally. My dad never stole anything. He was an honest man and I know that because although his close mates called him Tiddler he was also known as 'Honest Frank' Hardee.

Working on the river was a big family thing: a job for life in the days when people really did have a job for life. My family assumed I'd work on the river too, because I turned out quite bright – I got the highest eleven-plus exam grade at my school. As it happened, it was lucky I didn't have to go on the river because, in the late 1960s and early 1970s, it was discovered that it was cheaper to put things in big sealed containers and send them by road. River life fell apart and many whose families had been on the river for generations were abruptly made redundant. Some went to work on the pleasure boats; one of my dad's mates became a bookmaker; another worked on Greenwich Pier. Lots tried to get into related trades in the declining docks, but there was never enough river work to go round so people spent their redundancy money and did anything they could to get by. My uncle Ralph became a taxi-driver.

Like Nanny Hardee my dad was a bit eccentric too, and mum was an admirable foil for him. He liked to think he could do impressions and every time he got drunk he sang 'Thank Heaven for Little Girls', but it was the only one he could do. He sounded *a bit* like Maurice Chevalier. Except he wasn't French and couldn't sing.

As he had proved with the steam train, my dad loved a gadget. The early 1950s saw the advent in ordinary homes of washing machines, electric kettles and other labour-saving devices. Dad bought a Sweep-Your-Own-Chimney kit.

Our immediate neighbour at Grover Court was a Mr Moran but, naturally, we called him Mr Moron. He was a mild-mannered, long-suffering man, who worked in an insurance office and, like many others in those days, had a pencil moustache.

Dad unpacked his Sweep-Your-Own-Chimney kit in our flat and covered all our furniture with sheets but, for some reason, he decided that the best way to sweep the chimney was downwards from the top while standing on the roof. He said to Mum: 'Get down by the fire and tell me when the soot's coming and we'll catch it all in there.'

Mum sat by the fireplace for a quarter of an hour but nothing happened. Then there was a knock at the door.

It was Mr Moran, who was covered in black dust. 'A funny thing's happened,' he said. 'There's soot pouring down my chimney.'

He never found out why. He must have gone to his grave still mystified.

Dad was one of those people who, once they have set their mind on something, will carry it through come what may. One day he came home with some carpet dye. My mother had invited Mr Moran round for a meal that evening because his wife was in hospital, having a baby, and men never cooked for themselves then. Also, we were one of the few families in Grover Court to have a telephone and he was eagerly awaiting news of his wife.

My father set about dyeing the carpet while we were sitting down for tea. (Dinner was called 'tea' in those days.) Our G-Plan table was by the window and the door was at the other side of the room. Dad's idea was to dye half of the carpet while we had tea then do the other half later on. He began at the door, working inwards towards the window. He'd been at it for a while when something made him look again at the instructions. It was then he discovered that you couldn't tread on it for four hours.

At this point, the phone rang. It was the hospital. Mrs Moran was having the baby. Mr Moran, not unreasonably, wanted to get to the door.

Dad said, 'You can't! It's all wet! You can't walk on the carpet!'

There was a twenty-foot drop from our first-floor window to the ground. Mr Moran had to climb out on to the sill and we lowered him down with the tablecloth. Mum and Dad held one end – I tried to help – and Mr Moran hung on for dear life at the other.

Life in Grover Court was seldom dull. Someone used to steal underwear off washing-lines in the area. One night my dad was drunk and got up in the middle of the night to go to the toilet. He managed to lock himself out of the flat and nothing wakes my mum up. So he had to go downstairs and out the front of the block to get round to the back where he could get in. As he was walking round outside in a string vest and nothing else, he was stopped by the police, who were looking for the underwear thief.

He explained himself out of it in the end. Dressed only in a vest, he didn't exactly look like a very proficient stealer of underwear. But it was the talk of Grover Court for quite a bit.

Our flat was always full of Dad's mates. There was a close feeling of community among river people and they were famous for their 'beanos' – their parties and trips away. Each year, they went to a seaside resort in about six coaches.

Dad had a friend called Knocker, so-called because he 'knocked off' things. One year they all went on a beano to Margate and there were stories of people floating about in the sea with top hats and cigars and all that sort of carry-on. At the end of the day they were in a pub till last orders at eleven o'clock and Dad and Knocker were a bit the worse for drink. They saw another mate called Ginger – his second name was Baker – in the pub and started chatting to him. All three of them proceeded to get more and more drunk. By closing time, Ginger was the worst but Dad said kindly: 'Don't worry, Ginger! We'll get you home.'

He and Knocker helped their incapable companion on to the coach and were driven from Margate to Rotherhithe in South East London. It was about two o'clock in the morning when they reached his home. They took Ginger up to the third floor of the council block where he lived and rang the bell. His fourteen-year-old daughter came to the door. 'Hello,' Dad said, 'we've brought your dad back from the beano.'

The girl looked at him as if he was mad and said, 'Beano? What beano? He was on holiday with my mum in Margate.'

My home was surprisingly cosmopolitan because although many riverfolk were not well educated, they met all kinds of people off ships from all over the world. They developed a cynical, worldly sense of humour. But they were patriotic too. We stood up in our flat whenever 'God Save the Queen' was played on the radio. But everywhere was like that then.

When I was born the Second World War had only been

over for five years, so everyone had patriotism instilled in them. 'Patriotic' did not mean 'right wing' in those days. Even in the 1960s if you had a Union Jack on your parka or you went abroad with a Union Jack it wasn't right wing, it was just eccentric. People with Union Jacks stuck in bowler hats: it was just eccentric.

In the 1950s and early 1960s river work brought in a good wage. Around 1960, I remember a figure quoted of forty pounds a week, which was probably about the same as a doctor earned. But even though the lightermen had good money, the way of the Working Man was to fritter it away. Although a doctor might be on the same wage he would save and invest whereas with a lighterman it just went. Much like myself today. I earn enormous amounts but it just goes.

Dad spent his money on good living and going out. He liked taking the car on day trips to the seaside. There would be me, the two grandmothers, Aunt Kit and my mum. We went to Devon several times. Once, we got in the car at Lewisham and drove all the way down there, parked the car by the sea, got out for about four minutes, then all got in again and drove back to London.

Dad didn't have flash cars, just newish ones. The first one I remember was a white Cortina and then there was a Corsair. He loved cars and driving and I love driving. Some people say stealing cars is sexual, that fast cars and the excitement of them replace sex. Then I just liked driving. I still like it now.

My family's interest in motors goes way back. My dad's father was one of the first people in Britain to have a motorbike. He even married my grandmother on one: she went to the ceremony in the sidecar. It was thought so newsworthy that a picture was printed in the *New York Times*. My mum still has a copy of the paper.

Ours had been quite a big family. My father's mother had four or five sisters and a couple of brothers. One of the sisters, Flo, worked as cook/housekeeper at Wilsford Manor in Wiltshire, now the country residence of the pop singer Sting. When I was a kid, we used to drive down there a lot and stay with Flo. The house was magnificent. The rooms were art deco but some had been left like Miss Havisham's in *Great Expectations* and others made hers look like Habitat.

Flo's husband, Lou, had a strong Wiltshire accent, much stronger than you get anywhere nowadays. I think people's accents were stronger in those days because they didn't have a lot of TV: television levels out people's accents.

Flo and Lou used to look after Stephen Tennant, the owner of Wilsford Manor. (He was related to Colin Tennant who owns Mustique, the island that Princess Margaret goes to.) Stephen Tennant lived alone, with the occasional boyfriend, in this massive mansion with its own trout river. He used the old stables as his garage – there was a Rolls-Royce in there that he never went out in. He had an aviary with parrots flying about and a summerhouse/conservatory which he filled up with lizards. Completely mad.

Sometimes I heard bells ringing in the house. He used to ring for his toast; he liked it burnt. I was a small kid and it all seemed perfectly reasonable. I thought Aunt Flo owned this place and that Stephen Tennant was just someone who rang bells. I think I saw him once in all the times I went there. He was walking across the vast expanse of lawn. He had very blond hair, probably dyed, and on top sported a Panama hat. He was very, very gay – but you don't understand what gay is at that age.

I saw Greta Garbo on the lawn at Wilsford when I was eight or nine. She was a guest of Stephen Tennant. I was lying on the grass and she stepped over me. I've had a few people step over me. I had the Laird of Cromarty step over me once at one of his houses in Blackheath and he had a kilt on. He wasn't wearing anything underneath. I got off with his daughter – sort of – but she insisted I slept in the spare bed in a room just by the hall. When he came round the next day to see her I was lying in the bed and he just stepped over me.

Once, when I was about ten, we were at Wilsford when some money went missing and I was wrongly accused of stealing it. It has always been one of my pet hates: being accused of something I didn't do – even though I *have* done lots of things.

I was totally honest until I was fourteen or fifteen: I was in the Scouts and went to church. At Wilsford Manor, I felt bad being accused of pinching money when I hadn't. It might even have triggered me off to do it later on. Sometimes I have wondered if perhaps I *did* take that money and blocked it out. But I don't *think* I did . . .

We had another relation in Wiltshire called Bob. He lived in a gypsy caravan near Aunt Flo and was always humming: 'Hmmm, hmmm, hmmm, hmm, hmmmmm.' As he got older, that's how he talked.

Then there was another of my grandmother's brothers: Uncle Sid. He wore a fez all the time. He was completely off his head. He never said why he wore a fez – never mentioned it. Well, he was bald and he'd been to Morocco: it might have been that. And he had a handle-bar moustache. He was the longest-living man in the family – he lived well into his eighties. Most of the men in my family have died young. Dad was fifty-four, his dad was thirty-four, and his brother Malcolm only twenty-one when he was killed in the war.

Dad left the river in 1939 to go to war. He never talked about it. I only found out at his funeral that he'd been heroic. He could have avoided joining up because of his work on the river but he was patriotic. He was a gunner in the Merchant Navy on the Russian convoys, which was particularly hard – freezing cold for a start. Lots of our ships went down in the icy waters.

It was just after Dad was demobbed that he met Mum in a pub called the Dutch House on the A20. They met on VJ Night. He was quite old when he got married – thirty-two – and Mum was twenty. They stayed rooted in South East London, with never a thought of leaving.

People think the East End and South East London are much the same, but they're completely different. In the war, the Germans had bombed the East End heavily. Afterwards the old community feeling disappeared due to redevelopment of the area and East Enders scattered to Harlow and places like that. I think in South East London they stayed in the bits round the bombed areas: the communities kept together and the criminal families remained intact – more so than the East End ones did.

In the 1950s South East London had a big wave of West Indian immigrants, whereas the East End didn't. London Transport recruited West Indians to two main areas where there were big bus garages: Brixton and Lewisham. So we had an influx of West Indians round the area where I was born. There was a Victorian house just behind Grover Court. It was one of the first houses painted up in West Indian style – pink, blue, green, every colour you could think of. The bloke who owned it used to sit out on the porch, as if he was still in Jamaica, playing a guitar – perhaps that's where Val got the idea from. He still lives there and the house, though faded, is still multi-coloured.

Then, West Indians were considered very exotic – a vibrant addition to Britain. There were Africans too – Nigerians. But as kids we were scared of black people: it was just fear of the unknown – that, and watching *Tarzan* films. When I saw my first black person, I remember bowing down and saying, 'Salami! Salami! You are barmy!' And running away.

A West Indian family moved into the next road and we threw stones at their windows. I smashed the window in their front door and they caught me and locked me up in their house. I'd never been so scared in my life. There were all these black people in this house and what seemed to me a very peculiar smell from their cooking.

But I had a couple of black friends too, called Tom and Jerry – those were their real names. They were the same age as me and

13

they lived in Grover Court. I remember them at my birthday parties. Their father was Burmese and their mother was African.

We also had a woman who used to go sleepwalking during the day, with her arms straight down by her sides. She walked along the pavement, down to the end of the road, and then back again. In her nightgown. She never said anything and no one ever tried to stop her. There was not a lot of traffic about then and we saw her when we were playing in the street outside Grover Court in the late afternoon after school.

At Grover Court, there was also a 'genteel' woman, sort of Edge of the Aristocracy. She'd obviously seen better days. A bit of snobbery in there somewhere. She lived at Grover Court with her son and I saw him again, years later, in Borstal where he was the assistant governor. He didn't recognise me and I didn't mention it.

So that was my South East London, the seedbed for my life that was to become a bit like a mirror of the Krays' over the river in the East End – except they did 90 per cent crime and 10 per cent showbiz. I managed to reverse the percentages – must have been a dodgy mirror.

CHAPTER 2

ONE CHERUB, THE ANGEL AND
SOME HOLY SMOKE

I was thought clever at school – my nickname, at some point, was 'Brains'. I wasn't a hard worker, because I found schoolwork easy. I think I was one of the brightest mainly because it was a fairly deprived area, so there were people at my schools who would now be described as having learning difficulties. I'm always at my best when I'm with people who are, well, thicker than me. At school I habitually linked up with the strong bloke – not with the school bully but with the one everyone admired. The good-looking type. I think it was a defence to save me from any bullying. I never, ever, *was* bullied. For one thing, I wore glasses from a very early age and there used to be an understanding that you don't hit someone with glasses. So no one would ever hit me. And having never had to learn to be timid I've never, ever, been scared of anything. Violence doesn't scare me at all.

When, aged eight or nine, I first wore specs, one lens was covered with soap in an early medical attempt to cure a lazy eye. It made matters worse, really, as my good eye was obscured with the soapy mist and my bad eye remained lazy. During one of our regular holidays to the Kent coast, I won my first prize. There was a clown/Punch and Judy man working on the beach at Ramsgate and he held Smokey the Clown's Fancy Dress Competition. I entered as Smokey the Clown, decked out in crêpe paper and wearing a ping-pong ball nose, and won first prize – a picture of Smokey the Clown! All thanks to a droopy, clown-like, lazy eye.

During that time, which was the heyday of the South Coast holiday resorts, big companies used to run promotions sending some poor bugger of an employee round a popular resort with a wad of cash. If you had, say, a copy of the *Daily Express* then you went up to their 'Mr Money', and said, 'Hello, Mr Money! I claim my five pounds.' And he gave you a fiver. The trouble was that most adults look the same to kids and a lot of my holidays were spent going up to complete strangers demanding money.

Perhaps that's why later promotions saw people wandering around in bear costumes instead.

Apart from Smokey the Clown, my first experience of showbiz was, like many people's, from gramophone records. At about the age of ten, John Griffin was my particular mate. He was good-looking and strong but not necessarily gifted with brains. I went round to his house and once played a Peter Sellers record to his dad who worked in warehouses by the river. It was an LP which I thought extremely funny and included 'Balham: Gateway to the South'. I remember John and his dad looked at me as if I was mad. They just didn't think *The Goons* were funny. It wasn't part of the culture: Mr Griffin was a pub pianist – 'Maybe It's Because I'm A Londoner', all that sort of stuff. He didn't appreciate irony or parody and, hence, neither did John.

John Griffin always got the main part in our school plays because of his classic good looks. If I was cast at all I was only ever on stage for about three seconds. I might not have been pushy enough. For all that, John ended up as a postman.

One year at primary school, I was in *Alice in Wonderland* as the Frog Footman. My big moment came when a bloke called David Briggs got meningitis. He was the Fish Footman, so I had to be the Frog Footman *and* the Fish Footman. It was off with the frog mask, on with the fish mask! And I was away – showbiz at last!

One reason I didn't get bigger parts in the plays was that my primary-school teacher, Mrs Pawsey, more than hated me. We once had to write an essay entitled 'This Is Our Teacher'. She was very thin, so I wrote something like: 'Our teacher is called Mrs Pawsey. We call her Old Pozzle. She's as thin as a rake. My dad was going to use her as a pipe cleaner . . .' When she read this, she got me out in front of the class, whacked me round the back of the legs and sent me out. About a week later her husband, who was also a teacher, came to take us for football. We were all queuing up ready to go off. 'Which one's Malcolm Hardee?' he asked.

17

'Me.'

And he beat me up in the street. Not just hit me – beat me up. I was on the ground. He went mad, kicking me in the side of my body and all sorts. 'You guttersnipe,' he said as he kicked me – and the way he spat out the words made me realise he meant business.

Afterwards, I went off and played football. I was a bit shocked. This was more than the usual slap round the back of the leg. I suppose I must have upset his wife and she'd gone home in tears. But it was satire, really, wasn't it? I guess Mr Pawsey's violence came from misguided chivalry. I didn't tell my parents because I led two separate existences: school was school and home was home.

I had a 'home friend' who was known as Wizo (not Whizzo), a shortening of his real name: Wiseman. He lived round the corner from Grover Court. I met him when I was about eleven and he became important in my life later on. He was a cherubic, freckled lad, a bit like Keith Chegwin to look at. He was three years younger than me, and at eleven and eight that's a big difference. The attraction of Wizo was that he was younger and therefore more gullible. He was up for anything I suggested. I was the leader and Wizo would follow anywhere and do anything to order.

The first misdemeanour I committed was at Grover Court when I was around eleven. There was a bike leaning against a wall behind our block of flats. I borrowed it and abandoned it with Wizo down the road. The owners found out it was me and came down to my school. I didn't know it was the local midwife's bike. We didn't see anything wrong with nicking it: it was just some bike left there by someone. It didn't seem criminal at the time – didn't seem *anything* wrong with it, really.

My big mate, though, was still Pat Sherlock's son, Barry – also three years younger than me. Later, when it suited me, I would claim I'd fallen in with a bad lot, but the truth was that *I* was the bad lot. Nearly every weekend we travelled up to the West End. A particular favourite was Leicester Square tube station, where we spent many a happy hour sliding down the hand-rails on the escalators. I used to come home with a big black streak right down my body. You can't do it now because they've put lumps on the escalator hand-rails. We used to lie face down, pointing uphill, then grip the rubber hand-rail and – whoosh! – down we went, one leg dangling into the escalator well, with the other balancing on the central partition.

We'd go straight from playing in the Underground to Soho strip clubs. The attraction was not that they were strip clubs, it was the excitement of 'bunking in' (getting in for free). We were so short we could run under the kiosk windows and get in without being noticed. I don't recall any strippers, just the music and the smoky atmosphere. Because we were so short, we ended up looking through men's legs and usually we were only in there for about two minutes before someone realised kids were around. Then there would be a hoo-hah and we'd have to leap out. To this day, I've always been attracted to strippers, though.

We used to bunk in everywhere. One trick was to send Barry Sherlock into a building on the pretext of looking for his mum. Then he would open an emergency exit door and hordes of local ruffians would pile in. I got into the London Palladium like that. Norman Wisdom was playing Buttons in *Cinderella*. I remember him throwing sweets out to the kids. Circuses were too easy, really, although I had a hairy experience once when we bunked into Chipperfield's, which had pitched up on Blackheath, no more than a mile from home. Our favourite method of entry was simply to crawl under a flap in the tent. One day, we arrived a little late. I wriggled into the Big Top and found myself right next to the tunnel where the lions came out. About three feet away from me was a monstrous, mangy old lion and, two feet away from him, a circus hand driving him into the ring. In retrospect, I was more bothered by the prospect of being evicted by the circus hand than mauled by the lion.

I've got a soft spot for circuses. We went to Bertram Mills' Circus at Olympia more or less weekly. One time a friend and I bunked in and found it was full but for two empty seats, so we sat on them. About three-quarters of the way through the performance an Italian couple I recognised came in and indicated we were sitting in their seats but, because they couldn't speak proper English, we said: 'Oh, no, we've paid.'

It turned out they were the stooges in the horse act. They put a harness on the man and the 'wife' chased him and her skirt came off and all that sort of thing. I'd seen the show before and had thought these people were for real even though I had seen them do the same gag four or five times – I'd thought, That bloke's mad to keep volunteering to go on that horse. Somehow the illusion was maintained because of the way they acted. After we sat in their seats I realised that they were merely part of the act and that it was all a bit of a con. An early lesson in life and showbiz.

Another favourite venue for bunking into was the Lewisham Gaumont for Saturday morning pictures. If it was your birthday they used to let you in free and then get you up on to the stage. The only proof required was that you should bring along a birthday card. So I got birthday cards for different Saturdays – but not every week. That would have been when I was about eleven or twelve – much older if you were to count all the birthdays I had celebrated there.

I was blamed for setting fire to the Gaumont, but I didn't do it. In those days, cinemas had little anterooms with sofas in. The innocent arsonist set light to one of those but the whole bloody place went up. It was a million-pound fire and our bunking-in had to stop when it was reduced to a pile of smóuldering rubble.

There was another cinema opposite, and after the Gaumont

went up, I remember seeing the manager of the Rex standing outside wearing a bow-tie rubbing his hands with glee. After the Gaumont had been refurbished and had changed its name to the Odeon, I broke into the Rex one day with a bloke called 'Fatty' Hodgkins and we set light to the screen. We ran out and stood at Lewisham station, above the Rex, watching the entire cinema burn and· all the firemen working to put it out. I liked the drama, I think, but I didn't want to see anyone burnt or hurt.

The next day I passed the Odeon, formerly the Gaumont, and saw the manager standing on his front steps rubbing his hands gleefully looking at the ashes of the Rex.

After the mysterious conflagration, the Rex was refurbished and became two cinemas: Studios 6 and 7.

Both the Lewisham Odeon and Studios 6 and 7 have now been flattened by bulldozers, courtesy of Lewisham Council, which is the pattern of the fairly recent changing face of Lewisham and, indeed, most London suburban areas. We used to have a colossal department store, Chiesmans, and the Army & Navy. They were demolished last year. Lewisham Market, where I had many friends, is still there, but they're trying to move the old traders into the ultra-modern, ultra-crap Lewisham Precinct development.

My first school – St Stephen's Church of England Primary School, Thurston Road, Lewisham – has been pulled down to make way for an MFI furniture warehouse. The school building also housed a Sunday School and a boys' club. Our headmaster was a sadistic Welshman called Mr Hughes and we had to sing 'We'll Keep a Welcome in the Hillsides' every morning at assembly – in the middle of Lewisham! He was very strict – he used to come round and hit you with his ruler on the back of your knuckles. Admittedly, we *had* done things we shouldn't have done.

In Sunday School, the back of the piano was covered with a black cloth. One day, my mate Paul Smith, who lived underneath me at Grover Court, and I happened to have a box of matches

21

and I remember lighting the black cloth. I think it must have taken some time for the fire to take hold because we were back in the general group and singing 'All Things Bright and Beautiful' before anyone saw the smoke. There were screams, but not from the woman playing. She was the last to see what was happening because the flames had to work their way up the back of the piano and over the top. It was members of the audience who screamed and we just ran. Afterwards, I confessed: 'I did it to see the Holy Smoke.' It caused a furore, but my mum says the Sunday School teachers continued to like me and asked me to tea the next week.

My co-arsonist Paul Smith was a polio victim. He wore a leg iron and had one of those tricycles with a boot at the back and a stick that came out so his mum could hold on to it – a sort of bread-bin affair. One day Barry Sherlock, with me and some others, tied Paul's leg irons and his feet to the pedals and his hands to the handlebars, put a load of petrol-soaked rags in the boot, set fire to them and pushed him down Lewisham Hill. He went down it like a rocket, screaming as he went. The tricycle stopped and miraculously he didn't get hurt.

It shows how cruel kids can be at that age, without realising it. We did it because it would look good, not because Paul had had polio. He was my mate, after all. I think I had an effect on him: he became an artist. For a time, he was my best mate and then he went to Australia. We swapped presents – he gave me his marbles.

I passed my eleven-plus exam with enough marks to be able to apply to a local public school, St Dunstan's, which is situated near Catford dog track. (I've always wondered, Will there ever be a Dogford cat track?) According to my mum, I didn't get into St Dunstan's because, during a disastrous parent interview, my dad came over as a bit of a rough diamond and didn't seem to fit in with St Dunstan's idea of what parents of sons who went to the school should be. When he was asked if I was any good at sport he said I wasn't. In fact I *was*. I don't know why he said that but

I think my dad might have seen me as a bit of an unsporty type because I wore glasses. The hierarchy of St Dunstan's saw him as the type who would poke his brush down the wrong chimney, in the wrong direction.

My failure to get into public school upset my mother more than me, because this was *the* top-notch local school, but I went on a scholarship to the local grammar school, Colfe's, which was also posh. I was the only kid from St Stephen's to go there. The posh kids didn't pick on me and I continued to mix with old friends from St Stephen's during the first and second year I was there. The work was hard compared with primary school – there was Latin, quadratic equations and all that sort of thing. Colfe's was a traditional grammar school where the masters wore mortar-boards and robes and flapped about the corridors like crows. One drawback was that obeying the school rules was paramount and one of the rules was that we had to wear full school uniform at all times, including a cap to and from school. Unfortunately, the Colfe's cap was navy blue with three golden rings, which made it look like a target, particularly if you were walking and your assailants were on the top deck of a double-decker bus. I frequently got pelted by the local Sedgehill Secondary Modern lads on their bus journey to school but if I took off my cap I was usually spotted by a master or prefect from Colfe's.

Now I was leading a treble existence. I had the posh school life; I was mixing with my low-life ex-primary school chums; and home was still home. When I was twelve or thirteen, St Stephen's held a summer fête. The headmaster had acquired two tickets to see the Beatles at the now restored Gaumont which he gave as prizes in a Guess the Number of Peas in the Jar competition. The night before Wizo and I wormed our way into the school and counted the peas. The next day, we duly won the tickets. I have no memory of anything apart from loads of screaming girls with scarves. I couldn't hear, but I saw the fab four.

I've since met Paul McCartney and George Harrison at Jools Holland's place. McCartney was on a path at the back of my garden because my back garden was bang next door to Jools's studio. I went, 'Oi! Oi!' to Paul, and he nodded as if he knew who I was. I don't suppose he did.

At school, although I was seen as difficult, I wasn't classified as wild, probably because of the spectacles. I certainly wasn't seen as tough. Puberty must have been my downfall; that, and the fact that I never got shot of the dodgy bunch of associates from St Stephen's.

My old primary school was next door to a Coca-Cola bottling plant. One of the first crimes we committed was to climb over the wall and swipe all these bottles of Coke. We drank them and that was that. We broke in there daily. After about forty times, I was arrested because they had set up a watch. They saw us and I was chased by a policeman. I ran behind a locksmith's and was climbing over a barbed-wire fence when the copper grabbed my leg, pulled it, and I gave up. He took me into the locksmith's, Willet & Son, where I was incarcerated in the workshop while they called for a police car. (The locksmith's is still there, an anachronism on the edge of Lewisham's shopping complex.)

I ended up in Greenwich Juvenile Court where, as a pupil of Colfe's, I was treated leniently. I was given a conditional discharge and a five-shilling fine.

Part of the Coca-Cola plant subsequently became a Solex carburettor factory and, at Colfe's, we'd been doing experiments on how to make hydrogen. I knew that if you put iron filings into hydrochloric acid you got hydrogen and I knew that hydrogen made things float. In the back yard of the factory were some big acid carboys – large jars – full of hydrochloric acid. They were wrapped up in metal frames with straw between them. Next to these were loads of metal shavings where screws had been manufactured. Big tubs of them. To show off my new-found intellectual

24

prowess in front of my lowly St Stephen's hooligan mates, I decided that, under my scientific direction, we would make a hot air balloon.

We scrambled into the factory and put the metal shavings into the acid carboys and hauled a tarpaulin over the top to try to make it float as all the hydrogen was belching out. In the meantime, an old fellow was riding past on a pushbike, smoking a fag, which he threw into the yard. The whole thing blew up. Big explosion. Metal bars flew out and stuck in the wall behind me. The ancient cyclist was blown off and flung right across the road. All I suffered was a cut under my chin from a bit of flying glass. I'm lucky to be alive really. I was only about five feet from the carboy. I wandered home and before I knew it there were firemen coming up the path. Dad went a bit mad about that: fire engines parked outside our house. I still have the scar under my chin.

Opposite St Stephen's and the Coca-Cola plant was a derelict pub called the Angel and, of course, we played there as well. One day, we knocked some bricks out of the wall of the pub into the warehouse next door and discovered it was full of fishing-tackle. I liked fishing at that time and to be inside the warehouse was like a dream come true: rods and reels everywhere. We systematically emptied the warehouse until the school caretaker grassed me up because he'd seen me on the roof of the pub. This time the police came round to Grover Court to search it but the only place they didn't look was under my bed where I'd put all the stuff.

During this year of many encounters with officialdom, I once unbelievably told the police that my dad had died in a lorry accident because I didn't want them round at the house again. Of course, they went straight there and said to him: 'You're meant to be dead in a lorry accident.'

The police were constant callers. My dad *must* have been shocked because he was 'Honest Frank' Hardee.

Until about the mid-1960s, like almost everyone in Grover

Court, my parents went to St Stephen's Church. After that, no one seemed to go to church much any more. It was a social thing. People went to church because that was what everyone did. I went to three churches every Sunday. The sermons were the boring bits – I liked it when they got a good hymn going so I could sing. I went to the St Stephen's early-morning mass. It was an Anglo-Catholic church: 'Anglo-Catholic' meant they were basically Church of England but with lots of stuff that Catholics do. It was in Latin and they had Confession. Then I would go to a low-life church: the Shrubbery Hall Mission. It used to take in tramps and dossers. One particular tramp must have been an actor in his time because he quoted Shakespeare, some of which I knew from school. He did Portia's speech from *The Merchant of Venice* – something about rain upon the bough beneath. Quoted it word for word. After the Shrubbery Hall Mission, at about six, I went to a West Indian church, which was brilliant. They used to give me a tambourine – me and my mate – and we used to sit at the back and join in all the gospel songs. I would sing 'Go Tell It on a Mountain' with the West Indians just as enthusiastically as I had been singing 'Kyrie Eleison' with the Anglo-Catholics in the morning.

I was a chorister at St Stephen's but by the age of thirteen or fourteen I had been thrown out and ended up going to yet another church in Catford to join their choir.

At fourteen, I had finally outgrown my St Stephen's luminaries and had started attracting an even rougher element, most of whose names it suits me to forget. We progressed from ransacking commercial premises and went private. I broke into a house with Chris Hawkins, one of my new-found accomplices. The house belonged to an old music-hall entertainer and we nicked his banjo, which was his pride and joy. Someone had seen us breaking in and they told old Mr Variety, so he came round to ask for his banjo back. We had already sold it for a fiver in a place called the Swap Shop about two miles away. Not only had we sold it, we'd spent the money, so, that night, we broke into the Swap Shop. There was thousands of pounds' worth of stuff in there. We retrieved the banjo *and* as many guitars as we could cart away in a barrow. We sold the guitars at school and gave the old man his banjo back, so everyone was happy except the owner of the Swap Shop. But as he had given us a fiver for the banjo then marked up about forty quid on top of it he deserved what happened to him.

I went into the Swap Shop the day after the night before and found a woman there, an oldish woman.

'We had a robbery here,' she remarked.

'That's terrible,' I said sympathetically, as I often would in the next few years.

Somehow, I couldn't but feel a bit guilty about old Mr Variety. Poor bugger – that banjo was probably all he had in the world. But I hadn't known that. Hardly knew him at all. I wouldn't have done it if he'd been a friend or a close acquaintance. I wouldn't steal from a friend: it's personal then.

The first record I ever bought was 'Deck of Cards' by Wink Martindale. It was covered by Max Bygraves later on. A right sloppy old song. A sentimental, religious thing, recorded in a church: 'When I see the Ace it reminds me there is one God . . .' It's about a soldier who doesn't need a Bible because he's got this pack of cards which reminds him of the fundamentals of morality and religion. A load of old bollocks, really. But I used to listen to it time and time again. It was the religious element that appealed to me. I must have been religious at the time, because I was confirmed. And I was very sentimental.

Religion had a few pay-backs too, which made it attractive once the sentiment had worn off. When I was in the choir at St Stephen's, I had a surplice and I used to wear it to go carol singing and earn some money at Christmas. I used to take a tuneless gang round with me. We'd visit all the posh houses in Blackheath carrying candles and all the right props. People would invite us in and put us on tape recorders to sent to their relatives. They thought the money was for the Church, of course.

I used to make money all year round. From early October until 5 November it would be the Penny-for-the-Guy routine then, once November had gone, I started up the carol singing. The rest of the year, we went round in Boy Scout uniforms and did Bob-a-Job. No one knows when Bob-a-Job Week actually is, so you can do it whenever you like. The only occasion it nearly brought us grief was when we called at a scoutmaster's house. He knew it wasn't Bob-a-Job Week but I explained to him I was in a different branch of the Scouts and it was *our* Bob-a-Job Week. I was not a Baden-Powell Scout but part of a splinter-group called the BBS (British Brotherhood of Scouts). The Baden-Powell Scouts' motto is 'Be Prepared', the BBS one was 'Always Ready'. Everything was almost the same but not quite. We still wore the uniforms and had the Scout oath and ran flags up the pole and all that business.

When I saw my BBS scoutmaster years later, it was obvious that he was gay but at the time he was just a scoutmaster to me. People weren't so aware of gayness then. I've never had any homosexual experiences but they must have been going on around me. Certainly my scoutmaster didn't fancy me: he just used to hit me with ropes every now and again. He used to like hitting people with ropes. I think he must have got chucked out of the Baden-Powell lot for some sexual scandal. We called him 'Bosun'; we had three scoutmasters: Bosun, Beaky and Kim.

Eventually I was thrown out of the BBS for writing fake notes from my mother to avoid going to a camp. I was no angel. I was thrown out of the choir. I was thrown out of everything, really.

Apparently I had been expelled from primary school. I don't remember it – I was too concussed. There was a set of stairs at the school and I used to leap up to hold on to a ledge and swing above them. I swung up but something went wrong and I fell on my head and woke up in Lewisham hospital. I had to stay in for three or four days. They discharged me early because I was going berserk – racing about in the wheelchairs in the ward. So I was thrown out of hospital too.

I don't think the concussion had any lasting effect on me, but both my mother and grandmother always thought it had, because that seemed to be the turning point in my behaviour.

In time I would be expelled from grammar school, too.

Just as I had been made to suffer a Welsh headmaster at St Stephen's, at Colfe's I faced another Welsh teacher called Mr Davis. We called him 'Joe' Davis – after the champion snooker player of the time – and if you did wrong with him he used to stand you out in front of the class and just cuff you as hard as he could round the side of the head with his hand. On your ear. It really hurt.

Another one was Mr Dakum. His thing was hitting your bottom with a slipper, but he used to warn you when he was going to do it. When I was due for the slipper I borrowed everyone's PE shorts. I would wear about nine pairs under my trousers and he used to bend me over the desk in front of the entire class who knew that I had these PE shorts on. As he was hitting me I would pretend it was hurting – 'Ooh! Aaahh!' – and wink at my audience. I know that he knew. He touched my bottom to feel if there was any padding there but he didn't say anything.

Colfe's had always been a posh grammar school even though it had been rehoused in prefabs after the war before being moved from Lewisham to a brand new school in Lee. This site was very grand and the *pièce de résistance* was the Great Hall, with a window designed by Sir Basil Spence, who had something to do with Coventry Cathedral. In the Great Hall, they had a brand new organ on which the organist played at the front of the hall but the sound was piped from the back. I had a friend called 'Stinks' Newman, who was good at chemistry. Somehow we had got our hands on a railway detonator that we had prised off a track. When the trains went past certain places they ran over these detonators which made a bang to warn someone down the line of the train's approach. We used to liberate loads of them and set them off.

At the opening of the new school building the organ was being played to its full pomp. 'Stinks' had rigged it up so that when the pedal played B flat, a detonator would go off behind the pipes. As we were all singing the school song,

'Come, sons of Colfe's,

Come one and all

Tell out in lusty song

The stirring deeds of heath and

field . . .'

on the word 'field', the bloody thing exploded and one of the pipes – a big one about twenty feet high – lurched slowly out from the wall. A full hall. The mayor and all the dignitaries were there. And this big pipe was gradually tilting forward; it would have killed someone if it had fallen, but it didn't.

The school found out I was one of the plotters. 'Stinks' Newman *wasn't* expelled. Admittedly it had been my idea, but 'Stinks' was the one who rigged the thing up. Aged fourteen, I was expelled from school again.

I went from the semi-public-school regime of Colfe's, to Sedgehill Comprehensive. It was mixed-sex and the roughest school in the area – they even had race riots there. The deputy head was a hard bloke called Mr Dawson, who moved on to be headmaster of Eltham Green School: he was the headmaster who expelled

Boy George and remarked on his report 'This boy will never get anywhere.'

Even though I hadn't worked hard at my grammar school, when I arrived at Sedgehill, I was in the top stream straight away, way ahead of most people. I was a genius. Everything we were doing I'd done a year before, so I did hardly any work there at all. I took a lot of time off and spent days hanging around in cafés, playing on pinball machines and stealing motor scooters.

In the art class, we made smoke bombs by cutting up ping-pong balls, then wrapping them in silver paper. If you poke a bit of the ball out of the silver paper and set light to that, it burns with quite a flame. Then you blow it out and one ping-pong ball will fill a normal size classroom with smoke. We used to put them in tins of powder paint, resealing the lids afterwards. Eventually the tin lids would blow off – well, explode – and a lot of the powder would come out as well and there would be some powder-paint colour in the smoke.

At Sedgehill one master called Mr Garrett was notorious for never reading sick notes. I used to write my own:

Dear Mr Garrett,

I'm sorry Malcolm couldn't come into school, but he's had a dose of leukaemia.

Mrs J. Hardee

31

One day he read one of the notes. It said I had beri-beri. I was caned for that.

My parents never used corporal punishment on me. I think my dad hit me once with a little toy golf club. I don't hit my children. I slapped my son's hand once. With children, it's good enough just to raise your voice and they'll know. I think corporal punishment, generally speaking, is a bad thing. It can affect different people in different ways, but I'm sure a lot of the murderers and hard villains about today had violence inflicted on them to start with. Some of the people I later met in prison had appalling stories – normally not so much of harm at school but from the parents at home.

After less than a year at Sedgehill, when I was still only fifteen, I was expelled for being a nuisance and disruptive. I was still stealing scooters and, when I could be bothered, arriving at school on them.

Although Sedgehill expelled me, they let me come back to sit my O Levels, which I did in my pyjamas as some sort of protest. It was 1966 and coming up to the Summer of Love and you were allowed to wear your own clothes in that O Level year. I explained that my pyjamas *were* my own clothes. They were like those heavy blue and white striped jobs you used to be issued with in the army and I suppose they looked as if they could have been some Indian fashion. With my pyjamas, I wore suede Hush Puppies, socks and a mod parka jacket. I took the parka off before I went into the exam. I didn't want to look silly.

I passed four O Levels then – they would only let me take four – maths, English literature, English language and art. A little later on I passed a lot more – in less liberal institutions.

By the time I was expelled for the second time from secondary school, I had a modest criminal record that included the conditional discharge for stealing Coca-Cola. I often hung around a café at the side of the Odeon. It was called Botticelli's, but everyone knew it as Bottie's. It had a pinball machine and bagatelle, so became the focal point of some of the local youths' lives as well as those of these older villains who called me 'Brains'. I couldn't have been that brainy because they used to send me out to C&A to pinch clothes to order, and I was once caught lifting a pair of trousers. They were maroon and slightly flared. I stole trousers by going to the changing room to try them on, then putting my own trousers over the top. The trouble was that these maroon trousers were slightly longer than my own because the guy who wanted them was a bit taller than me.

For fun and variety I sometimes used to shop with my mother and pretend *she* was nicking stuff off the shelves. I would sidle up to the till and say: 'You know that's Doris the Dip, don't you?'

She actually got arrested once – well, stopped – in Chiesmans. She's always been indecisive, picking things up and putting them back and, with me standing behind her, she looked very suspicious. She said she had never felt so insulted in her life. But my mother has a sense of humour. I suppose she's had to have.

CHAPTER 3

WOLF G. HARDEE AND HIS MOBILE FUNCTIONS

My first proper girlfriend was Pamela Crew. I lost my virginity on my sixteenth birthday. So did she, although it wasn't her sixteenth birthday. Pretty quickly we were engaged but it was an up-and-down relationship. I bought her a ring and then we had a row on a 94 bus. I wasn't used to rows, but she was. She threw the ring back at me and I lost it. She never believed me: she thought I'd sold it, but I hadn't. I was engaged from the age of sixteen right through to about twenty and I was faithful to her. We were almost exactly the same age. She was a nice girl: she went to Prendergast, which was the sister school to Colfe's.

After we'd been together about six months, we learnt to exploit her father's regular habits. A builder, he was the nearest South East London could manage to Alf Garnett; a disappointed man because he wanted a boy and Pamela was one of four daughters. His routine was that he'd do his day's building then, at eight o'clock, go round to the Summerfield Arms at the end of their street. Every night he'd come home at eleven-fifteen and go to bed. I used to visit Pamela when he was out and sometimes we'd have sex in the front room when her mother and her younger sisters had gone upstairs.

One night, her father came back at ten-fifty and looked in. I was lying on top of Pam on the floor in front of the fire, banging away. He shut the door behind him and she went out and talked to him. She was in tears and he said to me: 'You've made your own bed, now you can lie on it!'

I didn't like to point out that we didn't use a bed.

Her mother always had a soft spot for me, but her father thought I was mad and alien. I went round there once on a white horse which I had taken from Mottingham Riding Stables. I thought, This will impress Pamela, but her dad answered the door.

'Hello,' I said. 'Is Pam in?'

He said, 'Bugger off, you silly fucker.'

And that was that.

I took the horse up to Blackheath and left it tethered to a tree. There was a piece in the *South East London Mercury* later that week, headed THE MYSTERY OF THE WHITE HORSE.

I once got Pam on the front page of the local paper as 'Miss June'. It was in the days before feminism and she was sitting in the swimming baths with her tits half hanging out. That impressed her – that I'd contacted the press.

I was sixteen when I left school, after taking my O Levels in 1966, and my first job was at a thriving advertising agency called Saward Baker at 79 New Cavendish Street in the West End. I started working as a messenger, as people did in those days – thinking you were going to progress up the line and become Mr Big at the top. I definitely wanted to be in advertising. It was a glamorous profession. We all wanted to be copywriters or advertising executives. I was the bee's knees, working in the West End: Malc the Mod, earning my living. My first weekly wage packet contained seven pounds, six shillings and eight pence (enough to buy half a suit in 1966).

At the ad agency I worked with a spotty youth called Rod Stewart, *not* Rod Stewart the singer. Like me, he was a messenger and a Mod and he had his own motor scooter. We were once stopped by the police going back to where he lived in Pratt's Bottom, near Orpington in Kent. The policeman asked him his name.

'Rod Stewart,' he said.

'Oh, yeah?' said the copper. 'Where do you live?'

'Pratt's Bottom.'

We were almost arrested on the spot.

One hot summer day, we went over to Regent's Park for the lunch hour. I had a platonic friend called Diane Ainsley, who was going out with a lad called Ray, and he came too. We were lying on the grass and I had turned over on my front to get a bit of suntan when he threw a knife in my back. It probably went about half an inch into my flesh and stuck there.

I was a bit shocked. He just *did* it – completely without emotion. He didn't say anything and I didn't ask why he'd done it because he was known to be a bit weird. He must have removed the knife and gone away. It didn't hurt. When I got back to work everyone asked what had happened because I was bleeding all over the place. My white shirt was scarlet. The first-aid kit was dug out and someone stuck a plaster on me.

On another occasion, I was sitting on a tube train with Ray. All of a sudden he got up and tried to deliver a karate kick right into the middle of my face, missed – narrowly – and sat down again. Never said anything. He just went like that occasionally. He lived in Blackheath and he was probably the first violent psychopath I had met. He wasn't a friend of mine. Just someone who was about. About to stab me. About to kick me. I've heard about him from time to time since then and there have been stories of shotguns . . .

Pamela Crew's best friend, June French, married Ray – at least, she had a baby by him. Diane Ainsley also had a baby by him. She must have been fourteen or fifteen at the time and had to go to a hostel for unmarried mothers. I met her again recently. She now lives in a picturesque little village in Kent. She married a Ray lookalike and seems very content. I saw her thirty-year-old daughter by Ray and quite fancied the daughter . . .

At the advertising agency, much as I wanted to be a copywriter I never got beyond being a messenger because I was sacked the first time I was drunk. I had about four pints of cider in the local pub and wanted to fight everyone, including the office manager, Mr McKenzie. I rolled back after lunch and said, 'Let's beat up Mac!'

I was one cocky, spotty sixteen-year-old messenger boy. And

I was swinging punches wildly round the room. I didn't hit Mr McKenzie. I was just a stupid young kid swinging punches. So I received my marching orders. But in those days when everyone was some sort of swinger, it didn't matter if you were sacked or lost your job because you could get another one the next day. Everything seemed possible.

In 1967, the Summer of Love, when some people were sitting in parks in kaftans, I was seventeen, on probation, at work and a Mod. My adolescent home-grown music heroes were Geno Washington and the Ram Jam Band, but I got into black-American soul music. That's what Mods did. I saw Otis Redding perform in an Oxford Street club called Tiles, which was open at lunchtime. He was brilliant. A very exciting live performer. I saw Wilson Pickett and I saw the Stax tour in Fairfield Hall, Croydon – Sam and Dave, Carla Thomas and Lee Dorsey.

Mod drugs were amphetamines – Purple Hearts. I *have* taken them since, but I didn't take them then. I had a scooter and never listened to The Who. They were a Rocker band.

The film *Quadrophenia* rewrote history, really. The Mods didn't listen to white bands: they listened to black bands and Otis Redding. The Small Faces were a bit of an exception – Mods listened to *them*. But The Who were not a Mod band, certainly not in South East London. I remember going to see them at Eltham Baths and the audience was mainly Rockers: leather-jacket boys. I had a Lambretta SX200 scooter, the fastest model around. In fact it was so fast the back wheel came off twice because when it accelerated it came off its bearings. That's how I lost it in the end: I had to abandon it somewhere and it was stolen.

In Catford there was a club called the Witchdoctor. It was a club we all went to although they didn't sell drink. Downstairs there was 'Mr Smith's', a casino, but upstairs they had a disc jockey called Steve Maxted who was white but played all the latest American soul music. They used to get in black-American soul bands – and some white bands too. I saw Marmalade there, *and* I saw Tony Blackburn singing in a band. He'd come along because he was a disc jockey on pirate radio. They had Johnnie Walker. And Ed Stewart – I got on stage with him. He used to get people up – 'First one up here with a pair of white knickers!' that sort of thing. I jumped on stage with anyone at the drop of a hat.

During 1967, Goldsmiths' College in New Cross had an event called 'The Happening'. Spike Milligan was on, Pink Floyd, and some bands I'd never heard of because it was all a bit hippie-ish for me. The Modern Jazz Quartet was out in the garden. I had no idea who Pink Floyd were – they were just a bunch of hippies to me. They were doing this arty show to a marionette sort of tune. I took my clothes off and walked across the front of the stage, stark naked, like a puppet. Public nudity was to the sixties what streaking became for the seventies. Pink Floyd were probably too stoned to notice. I just wandered across. It did provoke a bit of a reaction – from that day onward they stopped having concerts in the hall.

In 1967, I was no hippie. I wore suits: I was a sharp, snappy Mod dresser although, briefly, in 1968, I went slightly hippie-ish – but kept the nice suits, double-breasted ones.

After the advertising career had imploded I decided that I wanted to become a disc jockey, but I only had about eight records. One of my first professional engagements was a booking from a flower stallholder who worked at Lewisham market. I must have played 'Return Of The Django' by the Upsetters about twenty times in the course of the night.

I was probably the first mobile disc jockey – certainly the first to advertise in *Melody Maker*. There weren't mobile discothèques then and, in fact, there were very few discothèques at all. In South East London there was the Witchdoctor and there was a place in Lewisham called El Partido, a Jamaican club. I never went there because the seeds of racism were being sown in those early days and a voluntary code of apartheid seemed to operate.

Throughout, Steve Maxted, the DJ at the Witchdoctor, was my inspiration. He wasn't like a DJ today. He didn't just play the records; he used to do a whole show. Once a year, he used to stick pins through his face. And he used to show blue films on an old projector.

I advertised in *Melody Maker* as:

WOLF G. HARDEE

MOBILE DISCOTHEQUE FUNCTIONS

The ad generated several replies and I did my first gig for eleven pounds at a youth centre in Potters Bar. My dad drove me there. He didn't think I had a future in showbiz, but he was my dad and he had the car. I still didn't have many records – about twenty by now. I played 'Judy in Disguise with Glasses' about ten times and, just to make it a bit more interesting, I held a dance competition. The prize was a trumpet which I'd nicked somewhere. There was a fight at the end of the evening – it was that sort of place.

My next job was at the Carlton Ballroom in Slough. The manager was old-fashioned – bow-tie, dance bands and all that – but there was another disc jockey there, none other than Emperor Roscoe. He was the famous highly paid pirate-radio disc jockey and I was the 'other' (snotty, teenage) disc jockey.

As my disc jockeying progressed I sometimes performed with the Bonzo Dog Doo Dah Band. Our paths crossed a fair bit on the London pub circuit – the King Alfred and the Tiger's Head, both in Catford, and the Tiger's Head in Lee. I turned up in local pubs when they performed and played the harmonica with them

41

and did a couple of little fills with them. I shouldn't exaggerate: I wasn't a fully fledged member. But that was the first time I came across Neil Innes, who was with the band and whom I've met a few times since – although, to this day, I don't think he knows who I am.

This was the Swinging Sixties and, like Liverpool, the working-class areas of London had recovered from the war and its deprivations. Britain was changing and I was changing with it. As a Mod, mohair suits became *de rigueur*. South East London had a strong contingent of Mods, as did North London and the more remote parts of East London, out around Dagenham.

The middle-class teenagers of West and North West London tended to be verging towards hippiedom by then – certainly by the summer of 1967. Hippies tended to be the children of more affluent parents, like the Crusties are now. Except for Blackheath near Greenwich, South East London, then and now, tended to be a lower-middle-class or working-class area. A Blackheath pub called The Three Tuns was *the* hippie pub in 1968–9, but I used to go there as well. It was a focal point for young hippies but only held a couple of hundred people, so, in the summer, people sat outside smoking joints. I didn't smoke dope but I mixed with people who did.

Areas change: my grandmother used to talk about 'dirty old Greenwich' but today it's thought of as a desirable area. Even Lewisham, which was very run-down in my youth, is becoming almost up-market. But some things never change. The south bank of the Thames, from the City to Deptford, has been a haunt of self-contained communities of villains since Jacobean times. It has always had a feeling of 'Them' and 'Us'. That's still the case.

I think I probably *learnt* my disregard for authority. I just can't get on with authority and institutions like the Government or tax collectors. There *is* a sense of honour among thieves, though.

Basically, you don't shit on your own doorstep. By the end of the sixties I had become quite well known locally and Wolf G. Hardee was having his fifteen minutes of notoriety.

There was also a short period when I started getting into fights when I was drunk. I once had fisticuffs in a pub with a fellow called Barry Clegg. I attacked him and ended up half strangling him over the juke-box. After I had beaten him up, he brought his big mates up to find me. I emerged and it looked like there would be one hell of a mauling. I was clearly going to be pulverised by this thug called Micky Desmond, who was a right fist fighter. I was just about to lay into him with no hope of winning when a mate from Sedgehill, John Sales, came up on his motor scooter, saw me, and shouted: 'Jump on!'

And I did. And we just got away.

I probably would have been killed by Micky Desmond. He ended up in prison for attempted murder, though on that occasion he wasn't attempting to murder me.

During these heady days, Pamela Crew played the part of the moll to my gangster.

Stuart Morgan was another local Mod villain. He was stocky and was always getting into fights. He was a big Charlton Athletic supporter and, I suppose, was one of the original football hooligans. He was revered by that crowd. There is always someone who is King of the Herd and Stuart Morgan was the man. Our paths didn't cross much until I saw him in Wormwood Scrubs a few years later, when he had learnt to play the guitar. He copied songs from *Top of the Pops* and he was awful.

There was a big fight between Mods and Rockers at the King Alfred in Southend Lane, Catford, in the spirit of the regular Bank holiday fighting at Brighton and Margate. All the Mods were outside the pub and the Rockers assembled on the other side of the road, across which people were throwing bottles and glasses. The Mods soon realised there were about five times as many of them as there were Rockers and started running at them. I caught up with some Rocker, looked at him and thought, This is pointless, and walked off. Evidently he thought the same. He just looked at me. It was madness. If I'd been with a gang I'd have been obliged to fight him, but the fact that he was on his own and I was on my own made me think it simply wasn't worth it. So I looked at him and said: 'Oi, oi! It's a game, innit?' We shook hands and I went off and stole a car.

The first motor vehicles I had stolen were the motor scooters when I was still at school. Then someone told me how to nick a car using a threepenny bit – how to wedge it into the fuse-box of the ignition. It was easy. In 1967, you could open Mini doors with a screwdriver or, if you were really sophisticated, go to your local car spares place and buy a key – FS 967 – which fitted most Austin/Morris/BMC makes. If the ignition was difficult, you could open the bonnet (from the outside), jam a threepenny bit between two of the fuses and – hey presto! – the ignition was on. You then got back in the car, pressed the starter button on the floor and off you went. I wouldn't have a clue how to steal a modern car, but villainy seems to have kept up with the technology because the sport is just as popular now as it ever was.

The first car I nicked was a Mini van. I never took flash motors, except for a couple of Jags, an Austin Healey and a Rolls-Royce. When I stole cars, it wasn't for financial gain because we never sold them. A couple we 'rang up' – changed the number plates – so we could keep them for a month or two. But if you steal a car you don't look after it so it breaks down, at which point you abandon it and steal another.

I didn't nick them to drive fast, necessarily. Just to drive. But through stealing cars I became more involved with proper criminals. To get into villainy you've got to mix with people of a similar nature, unless you're something like a forger. Then you don't want to mix with anyone, because that's how forgers get

44

caught – not through visibly passing money but if the police can backtrack to them. Most criminal activity is quite a social thing because if you have stolen goods you must sell them to someone. In South East London they all used to meet in a pub called the Sultan, and Lewisham Snooker Hall was a famous haunt. I don't know why the police didn't go in there one day and arrest everyone. It was obvious that was where they hung out. I knew that from when I was sixteen or seventeen – so why didn't the police? Same thing if the police want to arrest anyone for drugs, which they seem to be keen on every now and again. Why don't they just go to the Glastonbury Festival? Arrest everyone!

I was sent to a detention centre for three months in 1968 and Pamela nobly stood by me. She gained a certain status with her mates because at the time *Bonnie and Clyde* was a popular film. I had broken into the record department at John Menzies over a bank holiday weekend with a bloke called Brian O'Hara.

I was still living at home although home then was about two miles from Grover Court, in a three-bedroom 1960s house in Blessington Close, Lewisham, that my parents bought because they'd been left some money. It was like *Brookside*. We had gone up in the world. Michael Leggo moved in next door shortly after we did. It was a cul-de-sac and much like Grover Court – a bit of an enclosed community.

John Menzies was handy – just up the road – especially since I was a Mod and Brian O'Hara was more of a hippie. I took all the Otis Redding, soul and Tamla Motown records and he took Pink Floyd, Grateful Dead and Bob Dylan. We had no trouble cutting up the spoils.

Brian smoked dope which I thought was stupid. He had some dream about distributing our stolen records to the poor and actually gave away a lot to strangers on Blackheath Hill. The police stopped him. Then they twigged where the records had come from, arrested him and took him off to Ashford Remand Centre in

45

Middlesex. Fair play to him, he didn't grass me up as his accomplice but I went round to his house and stupidly left a note on the door saying:

> # BRIAN! WHERE ARE YOU?
>
> # GIVE ME A RING.
>
> # MALCOLM 852 8677

The police got hold of the note, came round to my house and found all the records. I don't know why I left my phone number.

I was taken to Ladywell police station and charged, then driven back to Greenwich Magistrates' Court, from where I was sent to Ashford Remand Centre for reports on my suitability for a detention centre.

I spent two weeks in Ashford awaiting trial. It was the most depressing place I had ever been. It smelt permanently of piss and disinfectant and an air of no hope permeated the buildings. It was my first experience of being locked up and the place was full of hormonally challenged sixteen- to twenty-year-olds. I was in a cell with two sons of East End villains, who tried to beat me up. Luckily I was physically strong and I knocked them out. I was moved to another cell where there was an extremely posh gent and we passed the time playing cribbage. My father came to visit me and we both knew I had taken a wrong turning somewhere, but it would take me another ten years to sort myself out. My father was very upset. In my own way, so was I.

Finally, I was packed off to a detention centre in Goudhurst in Kent. It was like a rambling old country house with a board that said BLANTYRE HOUSE. I said to the coppers who took me: 'It looks just like a pub.'

When you're taken from court, the police are in charge of you. When you get to the detention centre or prison, the screws – the warders – are in charge. On arrival at Blantyre House, the routine was that the screws said: 'Stand up against that wall!' Then they smacked your head straight into the side of the wall. I watched this through a gap in the door and saw them do it to the three lads before me. I was spared the full treatment because of my glasses.

Life at Blantyre House was hard. You had to get up at six o'clock to run about four miles with medicine balls under your arms, do press-ups and drill. It was like the army: 'Quick march! Slow march! Get in line!'

There was a swimming pool and on 1 May, whatever the weather, you had to swim four lengths. That day in 1968 was a cold one and the swimming pool had a thin layer of ice on it. Some sadist forced us all to dive in. They worked you like demons. I was given solitary confinement for two days, in a damp cell on bread and water, just for shouting, 'Bollocks!' at some point during a football match.

During my time in Blantyre House the gangsters who were thought to be untouchable were put behind bars: the Krays (Ronnie and Reggie). They only operated in the East End and their influence has been overstated. They led just one of many gangs. The Richardsons (Charlie and Eddie) operated in South East London in a less high profile style. The really artful ones, of course, are those you don't read about: the Frenches were well known for local villainy and drew little publicity. I moved on the periphery of all this as the mobsters were a lot older and in a different league.

Eddie Richardson was involved in a big shooting at Mr Smith's, underneath the Witchdoctor in Catford. It was an inter-gang affair. They all met down at the gaming club and someone ended up shot and bleeding from an artery. 'Mad Frankie' Fraser – the Richardsons' infamous 'enforcer' – hit a man who subsequently died and 'Mad Frankie' himself was shot in the thigh. He dragged himself outside and the police found him lying in a front garden round the corner in Fordel Road, Catford, where Aunt Rosemary and Uncle Doug – the ones connected with the train crash – were then living. His mates had left him there. A bit inconsiderate to the neighbours.

No one outside South East London knew about the Richardsons until they were arrested and there was all the publicity at their trial about them torturing people in a home-made electric chair. But everyone knew the Krays. As comedian Lee Hurst says, the Blind Beggar must be the biggest pub in the world. Every time you meet a London taxi driver he was there when Ronnie Kray shot George Cornell.

Some people say the Krays wouldn't have been big if there hadn't been the shooting in the Blind Beggar. But now people are getting shot all the time. In the paper yesterday a bloke was shot at lunchtime in a pub in Yorkshire. I suppose the Krays were setting a trend. They also had that showbiz aura about them. They owned a club; the actress Barbara Windsor was a girlfriend of Charlie Kray and later married Ronnie Knight who worked for them – and the Conservative politician Lord Bob Boothby, whose mistress was Prime Minister Harold Macmillan's wife, was having it off with Ronnie, the gay Kray.

The film about the Krays erred on almost every detail. I saw part of it being filmed in Greenwich, which was the wrong place to begin with. They'd done up a street to look like 1934 when the twins were born and there was a scene where Billie Whitelaw, as their mother, was coming out of a door. I was watching this scene with a friend as it was being shot. We were sitting in Lil's Diner, a local café, where a lot of lorry drivers go. The director was struggling: first an aeroplane went over, then a lorry drove past and then someone coughed loudly. On the fifth or sixth take he was satisfied: all was quiet, the light was right, the sun was out and Billie Whitelaw came out the door with this double pram with two kids in it – and one of the lorry drivers yelled: 'So which one's the poof, then?'

The director went mad.

Having the pop-star Kemp twins playing the Krays wasn't quite right, either. They were from Spandau Ballet and the Krays and ballet don't seem to go together.

My sentence at the Blantyre House detention centre was three months, of which you used to serve five-sixths. It has changed now: at the time of writing, you get 50 per cent remission but there is a move afoot to abolish remission. That's madness, though. Remission is all that keeps prisoners in line. There's no real threat that your sentence will get even longer if you cause trouble, because that can only happen if you commit another criminal offence and are prosecuted through an outside court. If you smash up furniture that *is* criminal damage, but they're not going to take you through the courts again for that.

As you approached the end of your sentence, the screws became kinder to you so you forgot about the harder times when you first arrived, and you looked at the poor buggers coming in and felt quite superior. A bit like when you're at school. It's the same feeling you get when you've been in any institution for a while and you see newcomers arriving.

Prison is like mime or juggling: a tragic waste of time.

As I write, the Home Secretary is playing up to public opinion with the Short Sharp Shock and Bang 'em Away theories. It doesn't work. The people who have been locked away are normally very sad. No attempt is made to find out why they have done whatever they did. Apparently it costs about five hundred pounds per week to keep a person in prison. Give that person a wage of three hundred a week and they won't go back.

I came out of Blantyre House as fit as a fiddle, unreformed, reunited with my mate Wizo and clutching a grant of about six pounds. I took the train home and stepped off at Blackheath station, dead opposite the John Menzies shop which I'd been sentenced for breaking into. In the window was a notice saying:

RECORD SHOP

MANAGER REQUIRED.

APPLY WITHIN.

Straight off the train, I walked in and was given the job.

In the shop were all the records in white covers that I'd stolen – I hadn't got all the proper sleeves – and they still had my writing on them.

An old lady was in charge. 'You know,' she said, 'we had a terrible burglary in here a few months ago. They came and took all the records from downstairs and all the fountain pens from upstairs. They made a terrible mess!'

'Oh dear,' I said, 'terrible, isn't it?'

Being a record shop manager was a good job because I was able to 'borrow' all the best records to continue my career as a disc jockey. I used to play a pub in Brighton called the Ship where strippers would appear between records. Wizo got involved as my assistant disc jockey. His job was to keep me company but he used to come and lift records from Menzies as well. I'd sell him one; he'd take out ten.

In 1968, when Wizo was fifteen, he fathered a child. The

mother, Pauline, was fifteen too. She was a domineering girl. She had the child in a hostel, then they lived together in a shed by the side of the railway track because they'd been thrown out of their homes by both sets of parents. Eventually she got a Church flat in Forest Hill. Wizo felt a bit trapped by teenage fatherhood. I stole another Mini, went round to see him and said, 'Shall we go down to Cornwall? It'll cheer you up.'

He said to Pauline, 'I'm just going out.'

She said, 'Can you get me some fish and chips?'

'All right love,' he said.

Wizo and I drove all the way to Cornwall in the Mini, finally being arrested down there for car theft (of another vehicle) and burglary. We went to Exeter prison for about three months, came out, stole yet another car and drove back to South East London. He hadn't said a word to Pauline in all that time.

He said to me, 'I'd better buy those fish and chips.'

'You better had, Wizo,' I agreed.

So he bought the fish and chips, went back to the flat in Forest Hill and said, 'Hello, love,' as if nothing had happened.

'Oh. Hello,' said Pauline.

'It's okay,' he said. 'I've got your fish and chips.'

She opened them up, ate one and said, 'They're cold!'

Wizo and Pauline didn't stay together. They were so young. She was only fifteen, poor girl, bringing up a kid, and she wasn't over-blessed with intelligence. Last time I saw her she was in a betting shop and she'd married an Arab. I asked how she was getting on, thinking she would be in Easy Street. Unfortunately, he was as un-wealthy as she was. Not a lucky girl.

Wizo, of course, had given her the slip. Fat Wizo was always good at escaping. Once, in our car-stealing period at the end of the sixties, we nicked an E-Type Jag. We shared it. We parked it a hundred yards from Wizo's house in a working-class road, where it stuck out like the proverbial sore thumb. Wizo came out of his house one day, climbed into it and the police were waiting for him. They chased him, so he drove like a lunatic, leapt out and got away by jumping through people's gardens.

A still greater escape came after we had pinched a Mini-Cooper and three of us went for a drink at the Grasshopper in Westerham, Kent. It was Sunday and I didn't know that pubs in Kent then closed at ten o'clock on Sundays – half an hour earlier than in London. We trundled down to the Grasshopper at about ten-twenty-five to find it deserted. It was a vast Tudor coaching inn with a balcony on three sides and a little stage in the middle. Standing on the stage was an amplifier and microphone. I was a bit pissed and went up to the microphone and started singing for a laugh. Then two biggish fellows on the balcony yelled, 'Oi! What you doing?'

So we ran for it, as was our wont.

Wizo ran out first, hopped in the car and drove off, leaving behind me and our other mate, Pete Watts. Westerham is all fields, so we nipped over a hedge at which point I lost my glasses. These men from the pub came up to the hedge and were peering over and we thought, We'll front them out, so we stood up – hard like – and they ran away.

That was OK but it still left us stranded in the middle of Kent with no transport. So we jumped back over the hedge and walked towards the village centre to see if we could steal another car. Then the police drew up.

For some reason I decided to speak to them with an Irish accent to fool them into thinking I wasn't the same person who'd been at the pub earlier on, even though I had on bright red trousers and was uniquely identifiable.

'Excuse me,' said one copper. 'Were you outside that pub earlier on?'

'Sure an' we weren't!' I said, in this big, horrible Irish accent.

They brought the two blokes from the pub to identify us,

which was where my luck ran out. Unfortunately, they were Maltese so my Irish accent didn't mean anything to them. They recognised us and we were taken to Chelsfield police station where I felt I had to keep up the Irish accent.

'My name is John Murphy,' I said.

'Where do you live?'

'Oh, sure,' I said. 'Fifteen College Parade, Bromley.'

They charged me with the attempted theft of an amplifier – I'd only switched it on! Then they gave me bail under the name of John Murphy, 15 College Parade, Bromley. I'd invented the address, but it turned out there was a *real* 15 College Parade and the police insisted on delivering me to it.

We duly reached the address and I said, 'Well, you can't come in because me poor mother's got a very dicky heart. Goodnight, Officer.' I got out of the police car, went up to the door with pretend keys and pushed it. By some miracle it had been left off the latch, so I walked straight into someone else's house, switched on the hall light and the police drove off nodding. I think someone was in, but I waited for the police car to go away and then came out, stole my second Mini in twenty-four hours and drove home.

When they gave me bail they had taken my fingerprints, so when I went back to the police station in Chelsfield two weeks later to answer my bail, they knew I wasn't John Murphy. They said, 'Oh, hello, Mr Hardee. We found your glasses in a field.' It was all right, though: I was found not guilty.

I was less lucky with the sentencing I received for a series of break-ins.

The players in this criminal enterprise were myself, Wizo, Pete Watts and Brian O'Hara, the hippie with whom I had divided John Menzies's record selection. We intended to go to a posh party at Hildenborough, near Tonbridge in Kent, in a stolen Ford Consul. When we arrived, no one else was around: we'd got the wrong week and they were all away. So we broke into the house and had piled everything we could by the door, ready to load it into the Consul, when the owners returned. We all leapt out of various windows and ran away. I tried to escape in the Consul, but the irate householder blocked the drive and attacked the car with an axe. I jumped out and escaped on foot.

Wizo and I separated and got clean away while Pete Watts and Brian O'Hara were caught. I remember running across a field and crouching down behind a hedge.. The police were on the other side with dogs. I picked up a clod of earth and slung it as hard as I could over their heads and they followed the sound of the thud when it fell, while I scuttled off in the opposite direction. I had to thumb a lift on the A20 back into Catford and made it to a pub called the Rising Sun for the last knockings. Wizo was already there – he'd escaped in almost exactly the same way.

Next morning at six-thirty the police were round at my house. Pete Watts had confessed everything. They said to me: 'Would you like to come down to the police station?'

'No,' I said.

But they took me anyway.

TIC (Taken Into Consideration) means you are not charged separately for every offence you admit to having committed. If you *don't* mention TICs, they can rearrest you afterwards and you can find yourself in the dock for them all. Pete Watts overdid it on the TIC front. He was showing off: he confessed to crimes we hadn't even committed. We were supposed to have stolen a car in Leeds at four-thirty and then another in South East London at five-fifteen on the same day. The police were clearing up their books.

The outcome was that we were all banged up in Tonbridge nick for about a week, before being transferred to Canterbury prison, while we waited to be sentenced. The four of us shared the same cell. It was only twelve foot by eight but we were young and we had some laughs. That week, forty-seven illegal immigrants, all of whom claimed to be called Singh, had been arrested at Dover and ended up in Canterbury waiting to be deported. They were put to work sewing mailbags with us. Every time one had a visitor or needed to be taken out of the mailbag shop, a screw would come in and shout: 'Singh!' All forty-seven would stand up while Wizo, myself, Brian, Pete and various others burst into song.

The other three were sent to a detention centre but, as I had already enjoyed the benefits of one of those, I was sentenced to Borstal.

CHAPTER 4

I CAME OFF DRESSED AS A MONK

Borstal used to be called Borstal Training and lasted from six months to two years or, for particularly nasty crimes, you could get nine months to three years. It was a terrible sentence, really, because you couldn't be sure of the date of your release. I went to an open Borstal called Gaynes Hall, at an old RAF camp near Bedford.

Pamela must have been a long-suffering girl – she had already heard the phrases 'Once bitten, twice shy' and 'Never again' after my other court appearances. Also, while I was in Gaynes Hall, I was two-timing her by writing to a platonic girlfriend in Leeds called Nicola Hildebrandt. 'Platonic' meant I'd tried and failed to shag her at a party in South East London.

Foolishly I sent both a VO (Visitor's Order) for the same month and, as luck would have it, they turned up on the same day. Nicola, who knew about Pam, turned up fifteen minutes earlier, so I told her to tell Pam, who didn't know about Nicola, that she was my cousin. However, as the visit progressed, it became obvious to Pam – who knew all my family – that Nicola wasn't my cousin and the two of them spent the last hour of the visit talking to each other while I sat in silence.

I stuck Gaynes Hall for four or five months and then got in with the chaplain. He decided to take some of the boys out to a retreat at a monastery in Newark. We were all dead keen to go – but it turned out to be worse than Borstal. The food was fine but the place was run by a silent order of monks. Very peaceful but it nearly drove me up the wall. There was a phone nearby, so I called Pam. She came up and we shagged like rabbits in the woods, which gave me a taste for the outside world again and I decided to escape.

It wasn't very difficult. I helped myself to a monk's habit, so I'd be more likely to get lifts, and underneath it I wore my pants and a pair of Borstal boots – which didn't go too well with the habit, as the footwear traditionally worn by monks is the open sandal. I thought I'd be less likely to get caught if I went North, so I made for Leeds and Nicola Hildebrandt. My second lift, unfortunately, was from a vicar's wife who asked me what order I was in. I mimed that I was on a retreat and couldn't speak, but she was suspicious and later phoned the police. She dropped me off in Leeds, though, and I went round to Nicola's house, knocked on the door and, when she opened it, said, 'I always get in these bad habits.' Of course I couldn't stay with her, so I went to her friend Margaret's house, where, sure enough, at six the next morning the police were at the door. I was arrested and taken to Armley jail. They had known where to look because I'd written to Nicola from Borstal and, of course, there had been her visits.

I was taken from Leeds to Strangeways prison in Manchester, so I could be allocated to another Borstal, a closed one this time. I was transferred from Strangeways to Wormwood Scrubs in London en route for a southern Borstal. The sad thing was that, if I'd gone to a northern one I'd have been out in two or three months, because they were so full then that they were desperate to chuck people out. The average time spent in southern Borstals was about fourteen months.

I ended up in Dover, which was a right 'hard nuts' closed Borstal on top of the cliffs. When you got off the coach, all these tough Borstal types were watching to see what you were like. I was right at the back, behind all these lads in mohair suits with sovereign rings, still dressed as a monk. They thought I was a sex offender. It took a bit of convincing to tell them what had happened but, in the end, I was all right.

One day while I was in this Borstal, the chaplain came to see me and told me my father was so seriously ill he'd only got six hours to live. I was taken by train to London, handcuffed to a screw. He was quite decent and removed the handcuffs before we reached the house. I went in to discover that my father had died about half an hour before I arrived. It was September 1970.

When I saw him dead in bed, Nanny Hardee was sitting sternly by his side. My mother was downstairs, overcome by grief. I was twenty and my sister Clare ten – she had been shuffled off to relatives. My baby brother Alexander was less than a year old and was asleep in his pram. Mum must have been going through hell. She was forty-two, had just had another kid, her eldest child was in Borstal, with no sign of getting any better, and her husband had died. What a start to the new decade. Later that week, I went to the funeral, in handcuffs again but they took them off so I could read the lesson.

My father had died of cancer. Every picture you see of him, he's got a fag in his hand – even at his wedding. In those days you almost *had* to smoke. It was glamorous and macho. The river people loved a fag – still do. I didn't start smoking until I got back to Borstal after my father's death. There must have been some psychological link. As a kid, we used to smoke wild rhubarb, a woody sort of plant. We used to hollow that out, put any old nonsense in it, smoke, cough and that was it. I never wanted nicotine. I might have tried once when I was eleven or so but it was horrible. I hated cigarettes – *hated* them.

The strange thing was I'd been brought up in a smoky atmosphere. My dad smoked and so did Mum. Perhaps I was rebelling by not smoking. I didn't drink either until I was nineteen. All my mates were drinking and smoking but I thought they were fools. You know what it's like when you're sober and other people are drunk. I can't bear it now when I go out and don't have a drink when other people are drinking. I still find myself thinking they're mad. But when you're drunk too it's all right.

I was released from Borstal in January 1971, the same time as money went decimal. I got a job as a sports organiser and entertainer at Grooms Holiday Camp at Great Yarmouth, Norfolk.

My first proper showbiz job. Unfortunately, I had to sing in the evenings and my repertoire consisted of 'Swing Low Sweet Chariot' and 'Maybe It's Because I'm a Londoner.' My only assistant was an old boy called Harry, on the pianoforte, with a reel-to-reel tape recorder on which the drumbeat was recorded. Probably the world's first drum machine!

I didn't wear a red coat but Grooms Holiday Camp had a song that went something like:

We get up in the morning

And have our breakfast

Just like the bride

And Grooms . . .

We all had to sing it round the table at breakfast.

The holiday camp, in yet another old RAF base – I was getting used to them – was a real *Hi-De-Hi* place, a family-run affair with chalets. Each year in September, they had pupils aged from eight to sixteen from a private school in to fill up the slow week at the end of the season. My job was to amuse and entertain these kids, with one other fellow, for seven days and virtually twenty-four hours a day. Remembering my old Scout training, I decided to take them 'tracking' in the woods and split them into two groups. The other fellow and I were a couple of womanisers, so we took all the sixteen-year-old girls in our group and left the rest in the charge of some poor little ten-year-old. We were leaving a trail for the others to follow.

We got our group back to camp at about three and waited. And waited. Five o'clock came, then six and then it got dark. It turned out they'd tracked for about fifteen miles and fetched up at a different holiday camp and had to be driven back, crying, in mini-buses. I was sacked as an entertainer and was made head waiter instead.

While I was at Grooms, I went to London to see Pamela. When I got to her house a light was on. I had a look through the window in case she was in there with some other bloke. She *was*. Oh, I thought, this might be over. Correct. She eventually married him. They were happy for twenty-four years but I heard recently that she got divorced in 1992. I told her it wouldn't last.

Shortly after Pam and I finished, I went to a party and smoked dope for the first time. I felt *so* way out of it. I remember thinking, This isn't very good. I can't do anything. I've smoked some since, but now it has hardly any effect on me. It's not the same with drinking. With drink, I feel in control. There's a certain point where I'm more efficient and more confident with drink, though there's a point after that where anyone's useless. I always have a drink before I go on stage – and sometimes I'm drunkish but only to that point where I can do my job better.

After I came out of Borstal, I went right off the rails. I was twenty-one and Wizo was about eighteen. One thing we did was nick a load of silver from a big house in Buckinghamshire. We didn't know where to sell it – we knew it wouldn't be too clever to take it into a shop – until we ran into a couple of lads we recognised from Lewisham Snooker Hall. We didn't know their names, but we asked them what to do with it anyway. 'We can sell it round Pop Stevens's house,' they said. He was a well-known fence apparently, though Wizo and I had never heard of him.

I had my own Thames van at the time – not stolen – so I drove us all to Pop Stevens's in the shadiest part of Deptford. When we arrived, two detectives were standing on a corner. I could see they recognised me but we carried on to Pop Stevens's 'house', which was actually a flat in a tower block. Wizo went up with the silver to do the deal while I waited downstairs. Sure enough the detectives came over to me and said: 'What are you doing?'

'Oh, nothing,' I said. 'Just waiting for my friend.'

'Is this your van?'

'Yeah.'

While we were talking, Wizo and the two young villains came down the stairs carrying the silver. And there was still some in the back of the van. One of the detectives said: 'We're going to have to ask you to come down to the station with us.'

'Oh!' I said.

And then one said, thoughtlessly, to Wizo, 'You'll take this officer with you and drive the van and we'll take the others in the police car.'

Before Wizo's passenger could get in, Wizo had driven off like a rocket over the pavement and away.

I was taken with the other two to the police station. I said I didn't know who Wizo was. I don't grass. And I honestly didn't know who the hell the other two were. After all the questioning, the coppers said: 'Well, we only want to do one of you.'

We were all denying everything, so they drew lots to see which one of us it was to be. They put matchsticks between their fingers and whoever picked the shortest . . .

It was me.

I got done this time for receiving stolen goods from persons unknown, from places unknown. They never found out where the stuff came from, so the people we relieved of it had probably stolen it themselves. It hadn't been reported.

I was convicted by the magistrates but they felt they couldn't pass sentence on me. In those days they could pass sentences only up to six months and they thought because of my record I should get more. I was in limbo: a convicted criminal without a sentence. I had to wait for the Quarter Sessions in Wandsworth, the worst prison in the country – always was and always will be. It holds recidivists, people the authorities consider No-Hopers. It's enormously strict – I had bread and water in there.

I was in Wandsworth at the same time as 'Mad Frankie' Fraser. Everyone in prison knew who *he* was and what he'd done. His biggest thing was that he would just hit the prison governors as soon as he could. He hit eight or nine of them. Back in 1951, he had hung Lawton, the then governor at Wandsworth, with his dog from a tree on Wandsworth Common. Lawton didn't die because the branch bent and his feet touched the ground, but the dog did. When I was in Wandsworth, the governor was a Mr Beastie known, of course, as 'the Beast'. Lawton had been a horrible man but the Beast was worse.

In those days, Silent Labour was the rule in the mailbag shop. We had to sew mailbags, eight stitches to the inch, in silence. One reason you see criminals portrayed in movies talking out of the side of their mouths is that, in Silent Labour, it was the only way to communicate with the person next to you. A sort of sideways whisper. You got used to talking that way. It was the most depressing thing in the world, sitting there for eight hours sewing mailbags in silence broken only by the odd click of scissors. One day, after about seven and a half hours, some massive bloke at the back stood up and yelled: 'Remember you're a Womble!' He was carted away and I never saw him again.

I ended up going to the Inner London Quarter Sessions without a barrister. However, 'Dock Briefs' hang around the courts on the off-chance there might be someone for them to defend. They're not that good because they're normally past their prime. I saw this barrister who must have been seventy-odd and couldn't understand a word he said – probably due to a combination of his plummy accent and alcohol problems. I thought, I can't have him defending me! But, as he was the only one there, I had no alternative.

When he got up in court, the judge couldn't understand him either. If I'd had an articulate barrister coming out with the full facts I'd probably have got three years but the judge must have taken pity on me after listening to this geriatric because he gave me a twelve-month suspended sentence.

At that time, I used to go out with Wizo, nick cars and do all sorts of villainy. I got caught again in Kingsbridge, Devon, in the summer of 1971. When our stolen Mini started to play up we nicked a Rolls-Royce. I always thought it had belonged to government minister Peter Walker, but he wrote to me in 1995 stating that he had never owned one. Whoever it belonged to deserved to lose it. He left the keys in it.

While we were in the West Country, Wizo and I went on a real petty crime spree and managed to live off the proceeds for several weeks. We met a couple of girls: Wizo copped off with 'Brenda Suspender', and mine was Annie, who found me repulsive because of my unfashionable prison hairstyle.

The four of us booked into a caravan site in Crantock, near Newquay. I registered under the name of Mr Werb ('brew' spelt backwards). We unloaded the car, a Ford Taunus that I'd actually bought, which was full of the spoils from various burglaries and cheque frauds – jewellery, car radios, even a photographic enlarger – and hid the goods in the bowels of our holiday home.

Wizo and Brenda Suspender were in one double bed, shagging all night, but I got nowhere with Annie. By the morning, I'd had enough so, at six-thirty, I went off with a can to get some water to make tea. As I walked the fifty yards from the caravan to the stand-pipe, I saw two detectives coming towards me. I had just turned on the tap when Detective One said: 'Mr Werb?'

I said, 'No,' and pointed towards the caravan which held Wizo, Brenda, Annie and what looked like the contents of Aladdin's Cave.

Detective Two made his way towards it and the next thing I knew we were in Torquay police station on our way back to Exeter nick.

If you were twenty-one or over, you ended up in the adult prison, otherwise you were a YP (Young Prisoner, who would now be sent to Youth Custody). I was twenty-one at the time but pretended I was twenty because I wanted to stick with Wizo.

We were taken to Totnes Magistrates' Court, the oldest magistrates' court in the country with a rather forbidding atmosphere: it still had shackles on the wall. You couldn't get out of the police car and go straight into the court as it was in a pedestrian-only area. No. You had to get out of the police car in the public car park some distance away and be handcuffed, then walk through the streets of Totnes. It was all very embarrassing and I devised a plan for escaping.

We had to be taken to Totnes Magistrates' Court every week while they gathered all the charges against us before starting committal proceedings, which took at least a couple of months. Every week, after the court appearance, the police took us back to the prison in a Black Maria and undid our handcuffs. Then we'd walk about five yards to the prison reception, where the screws took charge of us. Prison officers and police have a hate-hate relationship. Most screws originally wanted to be coppers but didn't get in and each service thinks it's more important than the other.

I noticed we got back at the same time every week – about four o'clock, at the same time as some of the screws went off duty. They would open the wicket gate – the little door set in the main gates – and walk out of the prison. When they took off our handcuffs, that little wicket gate was usually open. One day I said to Wizo, 'When they take the cuffs off we can just run. We're in our own clothes, so that's no problem.'

'All right,' he said.

After about five weeks of this – we were trained up and fit – the little gate was open and I ran. Wizo, the great escapologist, however, stayed where he was.

A policeman came after me but he was about fifty so I got away into a park opposite the prison. It was summertime and I thought I'd wait until it got dark then try to make my way to London. I hid there from four o'clock until just before ten. Then the police caught me in the bushes. I'd been reported as a Peeping Tom by a woman who'd walked past and seen me. I was arrested and questioned for an hour and a half. They were on the point of letting me go when they suddenly twigged I was the same bloke who'd escaped from the prison in their town.

I was convicted at Exeter Quarter Sessions and ended up in a holding cell beneath the court. I'd been sitting there, depressed, thinking, I'm twenty-one; I'll be twenty-four when I get out, for about an hour, when another fellow came in and sat opposite me. There was a bit of a pause. Then he looked up and asked, 'What you in for, mate?'

'Nicking cars,' I said. Another pause. Then I said, 'So what *you* in for?'

'Drugs.'

'Oh.'

Then he asked, 'How long did you get?'

'Three years.'

'Oh.'

'How long did *you* get?'

'Seven years.'

'Oh.'

There was a very long pause and he said, 'Ever get one of those days when nothing seems to go right?'

We ended up in the same cell in Exeter Prison. When I opened the cell door, he saw it was me again and said, 'You'd better have the bunk nearest the door – you're out first.'

67

By this time, they had found out I was over twenty-one, so I had to go into the adult bit of the prison and wear 'patches'. If you were an escapee, or attempted escapee, yellow patches were sewn on your uniform, you had to be accompanied by a screw wherever you went and you could work and eat your dinner only with other yellow 'patches'. As I was the only one on patches, it was tantamount to solitary confinement. And it shouldn't have been. It lasted for about fourteen months, during which there were, perhaps, two months when I had companions. One was a mad ginger-haired bloke, who had jumped out of a Black Maria on the A30 and broken his leg. The other was a man in whose cell they'd found a hacksaw.

You could apply once a month to come off patches. I applied every month, and every month the governor refused. He still felt I was a risk – and that I wasn't behaving ideally: for around three months I refused to wash or shave by way of protest.

I used some of my time to take some more O and A Levels. One of the O Levels was 'Spoken English', although I'd hardly spoken to anyone in months. When the examiner turned up, I could hardly remember how to talk but, even so, I passed.

The only time I saw anyone was when I went to church. I became a Catholic because the Catholic priest handed out fags and, if you were a Catholic, you got two services a day, which was the only time I could mix with anyone. I exercised on my own. I sewed mailbags alone, from eight o'clock until four with an hour off for lunch, which they brought into my cell. Once a week I got out to go to the prison cinema: even then I had to sit at the back on my own with a screw next to me.

Exeter prison was not a happy experience.

There was a prison officer there called Bill Lovett who, so rumour went, had worked in Dartmoor prison, where someone had thrown him over the landing. He had to have a tin plate put in his head, which made him quite mad. In those days if you were transferred to any other prison in Britain and said you'd been in Exeter everyone would remark: 'Oh, you've met Bill Lovett, then!'

When I first went into Exeter, he marched up to me – an erect, military type with a gruff voice – and said: 'Get away! Get away out of it! Get away! Get away out of it!' He was a bit like the Scottish prison officer played by Fulton McKay in the BBC TV sitcom *Porridge*. But he was slightly schizophrenic and I was scared shitless the first time I met him. He ordered me into the cell and then slammed the door tight and I thought, He's mad! About five minutes later he opened the door and said gently, 'Anything you'd like? Cup of tea? Coffee? Library books?'

So I said, 'Oh, yeah, I wouldn't mind a cup of –' to which he yelled, 'Get away! Get away out of it!' and started wandering off again.

Sometimes he was in charge of the mailbag shop. Now, the bottom line for a screw in any prison is to know how many people you have in any one place at any one time – the screws sit on a high pedestal with a blackboard behind them and whenever anyone comes in or goes out they're meant to record it. But Bill Lovett didn't sit on the pedestal. He marched up and down the mailbag shop, shouting, 'Get away! Get away out of it!'

One day, the governor came round with the chief, who's the second-in-command, an important event in prison regime, like a general inspecting his troops.

'Morning, Mr Lovett,' said the governor.

'Morning, sir.'

'How many in, Mr Lovett?'

Lovett looked around, paused and eventually said, 'Quite a few, sir. Quite a few.'

The governor tore him off a strip at that and he had to go round counting everyone – very embarrassing for him, I'm sure, but a nice break in the monotony for us.

69

The governor was ex-Army. He'd had half his face blown off in the war and he had a huge scar – but he was all right. I got put on report to him once. I'd bought some loose tea from someone in the kitchens and got caught with it in my cell. You're not meant to have anything in your cell, particularly loose tea which could only have come from the kitchen. I was taken to see the governor with two screws, one on each side.

'What's your name?' I was asked, when we were standing in front of him.

'Hardee. Number 594711,' I said. '711 to my friends.'

'Call the governor SIR!' they said.

'I didn't realise he'd been knighted,' said I.

He lectured me on taking the tea – I hadn't told him I'd bought it, just said I'd got it somehow.

'Well,' he said, 'if everybody did the same thing no one in prison would have any tea.'

'On the contrary,' I said, 'if everyone did the same thing, then we'd *all* have some tea.'

I lost a fortnight's remission for being offensive.

It must have been towards the end of my sentence, when I'd been taken off patches, that I saw a notice saying: GLEE CLUB THIS TUESDAY. Three or four of us turned up to find that Mr Dwyer, the camp church organist, was running it. One minute we're singing Gilbert and Sullivan numbers and four-part harmonies to 'Bread of Heaven', the next he starts passing round the fags. Word got out fast about this and the Glee Club was suddenly attracting forty or fifty cons. No one could sing but we didn't have a problem with smoking the free fags.

One week the governor came in during the break, on one of his rare visits with the education officer – who was also as camp as a row of tents. The only place you're supposed to smoke is in your cell, and only at certain times – so we whisked the fags under our coats and prayed they'd make it quick.

The education officer said, 'Hello, Mr Dwyer. How's the Glee Club going?'

'Very well,' said Mr Dwyer.

'And what,' asked the education officer, 'are you doing now?'

'Gilbert and Sullivan,' cooed Mr Dwyer.

'The governor likes Gilbert and Sullivan,' squeaked the education officer.

'Well, if he likes 'em,' said one of the surlier cons at the back, in a broad West Country accent, 'he'd better fuck off now, then, hadn't he?'

Eventually, I was dispatched to a prison called Grendon Underwood in Buckinghamshire. They wouldn't take you there if you were on patches, so the governor at Exeter had sent me into the main prison about two months before. Coming off 'solitary' had been almost like being released, but going to Grendon seemed even more so. You were allowed to go more or less anywhere you liked there, even though it was a maximum security prison, but I don't think there had been any escapes. They called it a 'modern' prison: it was 'liberal' and you called the screws, who had to treat you right, by their first names. It was a psychiatric prison, though not a prison hospital like Rampton or Broadmoor. Grendon had two main sides: Psychiatric and Education. I was in Education. It had a hospital too, which took tattoos off. A lot of prisoners applied to have this done so that they stood a chance of getting to a cushy nick. The reason they gave the authorities, though, was that if they kept them, they wouldn't be able to get a job in a bank when they got out.

I joined every club I could find. I was in the drama society, 'The Toastmasters', the harmony singing ensemble, even the bridge club. It was odd playing bridge, normally associated with old ladies and retired colonels, in these surroundings – a bit like watching murderers singing four-part madrigals. John Stonehouse,

71

the Labour MP who had faked his own death, was my partner. He had pretended he'd drowned in Miami to get an enormous amount of life insurance. He's dead for real now. Perhaps. But he was very good at bridge. Another first-rate player was a 'lifer' called Bob Gentles. He'd already done twenty-odd years. I think he was heterosexual when he went in but he was one of those people who've been so long in prison they turn gay. He was *the* prison gay, *outrageously* gay.

There was no bigotry about homosexuality in jail. When I was first sent down, it was still illegal and there were men in prison just for being gay – ridiculous, really, to punish gays by sending them into a prison full of men.

In most prisons the screws didn't object to homosexuality. It was just accepted. There was a high proportion of gay men, some of whom wore make-up and lipstick. They used to get jobs in the kitchen and take on what was seen as the 'women's role'. The overtly camp ones were a laugh – we used to give them women's names. When I got to Grendon, homosexuality had been legalised for consenting over twenty-ones, so there were fewer overt gays there.

I was called 'Tadpole' at Grendon because I worked briefly in the gardens where I found a lot of tadpoles, which I kept in my chamber pot. I never got any intellectual jobs – in Grendon I started off making mats, not for the floor but for *beds*.

I shared a cell with a bloke called Bernie from Birmingham, who had had his moment of glory as a TV star. One day, at the height of his fame he went out, got pissed, nicked a lorryload of rice pudding and smashed the lorry through a shop window. The accident did untold damage – gas mains ruptured, all sorts. He got three years.

Bernie was gullible. In prison, tobacco is currency. We had half an ounce a week, which was equivalent to a week's wages, and every week, I used to bet Bernie I'd beat him at *Brain of*

Britain on the radio, and I did – every week. He never realised I listened to it alone on Mondays before the repeat we heard together on Fridays . . .

It was at Grendon that I met one Dexie Doug Davies, a local lad – local to me, that is. Upbringing is probably the biggest deciding factor in how someone is going to turn out, but heredity must have an effect too. Dexie Doug had been adopted into a middle-class family in which his father was the conductor of a symphony orchestra. DDD, though, was a born criminal. He got tattooed – that part *had* to be hereditary! – and lived the life of a drug-wrecked villain to the full. Dexie Doug had the normal home-made, Borstal-type tattoos: L-O-V-E and H-A-T-E on the fingers, and all that. You do them with shoe polish and the needle you use to sew mailbags. You prick holes in your skin with polish on the end of the needle and it's there for ever – unless you have a skin graft.

You can easily work out where criminals are going to spring from: some of the council estates in deprived areas of South East London are obvious sources. If you're born into an affluent lifestyle with plenty of opportunities, there's not much point in stealing that I can see, although Nick Leeson and Viscount Brocket would probably disagree with me.

The irony is that successful criminals tend to keep their working-class standards. They still live on council estates even though many can afford to move into big places with the nobs in Ascot. The furthest they'll go is East Essex. South East London council estates are what they understand, where they've been brought up and they aren't interested in sipping Earl Grey in Claridge's.

As my criminal record lengthened, the police became less tolerant but I only got beaten up once, when they thought I'd done a big drugs crime. I hadn't, really. What I *had* done was break into a chemist's with Dexie Doug Davies, who *was* a drug addict. I wasn't into drugs so I nicked the aftershaves while he was rummaging in the dangerous substances cabinet. He virtually had

73

morphine on toast, that fellow. He took anything. And he's still alive – nothing short of a miracle! The extraordinary thing is that his habit doesn't seem to have had any lasting effect on him. He's just the same whenever you see him.

I remember he had a batch of suppositories filled with something that he took out and sold. I went with him to flog the stuff to a right seedy dealer in Harrow. He was the archetypal 1960s hippie and Dexie Doug swapped his dangerous drugs for about half a pound of dope – of which I got a chunk for driving him over. (As I didn't smoke it, I sold it for an enormous amount of money.)

While we'd been upstairs with the dealer, the people downstairs in the house had noted my car number – PAD 999G – and told the police. It wasn't long before the coppers were round at my place accusing me of selling drugs.

Back I went to Ladywell police station in Lewisham to await the Drugs Squad from North London. When they arrived, one of them began beating me up in the interview room. It was a local copper there, Ron Smith – who'd had regular dealings with me – who put a stop to it. He was a policeman of the old school.

When the police interview you, they normally give you the hard and soft treatment. First, the nice bloke says: 'Now come on, Malcolm. Just tell me and it'll be OK.' Then the nasty one comes in and starts shouting at you. Once they were short-staffed and one officer had to play both parts. One minute he was saying: 'Here, Malcolm, have a cigarette,' and then, when I said I didn't smoke, he shrieked, 'Have a fag, you bastard!' and tried to ram it down my throat. The oddest thing was that he went in and out of the room to change character.

One positive thing I owe to Dexie Doug Davies is that he introduced me to Madelaine Wood – a strict Catholic, who became my pen pal in Grendon and with whom I briefly attempted to go out on my release – and she introduced me to the world of her middle-class family. It was my first exposure to the proper middle classes – but this household was a touch eccentric.

To this day, her mother still has the Christmas decorations up from 1976: they never come down. The family lives in an old Victorian house in Eltham and, in the back room, there's an Aga cooker with a wall above it that has never been decorated. Visitors are encouraged to write anything they like on it and over the decades the family has collected the wise sayings of drunkards. In 1972, I wrote ALAS POOR YORICK and it's still there.

Once Madelaine went out with me wearing a cocktail dress and roller-skates. I had on a long Doctor Who-type scarf. We spotted some people sitting in an Indian restaurant, so she went to one side of the window and I went to the other. She held my scarf low down, where they couldn't see it and I pulled her across. The people in the restaurant could only see the top half of her body and it looked like she was floating past the window. Her mum's nickname is 'Moth' – short for Mother. Her husband left her quite early on – he fled to New Zealand – and in the photos Moth keeps he has a big handle-bar moustache, just like my uncle Sid who used to wear a fez.

Madelaine has three brothers. Kieron is one of the most irreligious people I've ever met but is the religious correspondent for Irish Television. Jeremy is a very straight computer programmer, living comfortably in the stockbroker belt, and Laurence is one of the country's leading experts on tropical diseases. All three are like John Cleese. They're tall and manic with that John Cleese manner. Being Catholic, they are constantly surrounded by kids. Each brother has four or five and Madelaine now has four.

Because of the Catholicism, I think Kieron veers politically towards the right. In the last few years, I've tried to get him interested in alternative comedy, but he thinks it's just a bunch of left-wing lesbians. Laurence is quite socialist, though, and Jeremy, the computer programmer, is quite capitalist. Moth and

Madelaine are apolitical, really, but they're strong Catholics: Madelaine is a member of the 'Pro-Life' movement and gives anti-abortion talks.

Politics has never had any great effect on my life. When I was a kid Labour seemed 'common' and the Conservatives 'not common'. A Mr and Mrs Minns lived near us, and at one election time to the left side of their bay window they had a poster saying: VOTE CONSERVATIVE while on the right another read: VOTE LABOUR. I wondered how they got on together. They seemed happily married.

I stood for Parliament in the important Greenwich by-election in 1987 when Rosie Barnes stood for the SDP and Deirdre Wood for Labour. Everyone expected Labour to win but Rosie Barnes did. I was supported by the Rainbow Alliance, who were loosely connected with the Monster Raving Loony Party. They joined forces for this election and I met David – Screaming Lord – Sutch, who was broke and living with his mum. He was ringing up from phone boxes trying to get his £500 deposit together.

The Rainbow Alliance was run by an old hippie called George Weiss. He had had a lot of money from his parents, who were in the jewellery and silverware business and he'd blown it by gambling and betting on himself winning these elections, which he never did. I think he's convinced that one day he *will* win. He wanted computer-based referenda and Peace and Love all over the world. He always wanted to be a 'personality' but never managed it. His idea of humour was carrying a gonk about – one of those stuffed toys that were popular in the 1960s.

George had come to my Tunnel club – more about that later – and he wanted Jools Holland to stand for the Rainbow Alliance in Greenwich. Jools wouldn't go that far but agreed to be my sponsor and George put up the deposit. I stood for election under the banner the Rainbow Alliance Beer, Fags and Skittles Party, and we got tremendous press and TV coverage because everyone thought it was going to be the last by-election before the general election. It was a good laugh, especially when I went to the count. The Great British Public's ignorance knows no bounds. It must be the easiest thing in the world to put an 'X' next to a candidate's name but some people had put ticks, a few had given marks out of ten and some had voted for them all.

I got 174 votes. I beat the Communist Party *and* the National Front, which takes some doing because there's strong support for them in the Greenwich area. At that time, the comedy agent Addison Cresswell was very left wing and was handling all the Red Wedge tours – comedy *artistes* and others grooving for Labour. He phoned me up and went mad at me because I was standing – he thought I might take votes from the Labour Party. In the event, however, the Labour candidate lost by a lot more than 174.

If I had thought more seriously about it, part of my manifesto could have won the seat for me. This was 'Bring Charlton Athletic back to the Valley'. Charlton is the local football club and the Valley was their ground. At the time, they had to play at Crystal Palace's ground. If I had got the whole of the Charlton Football Supporters' Club on my side, I would have got enough votes to win. Four years later, they formed a Valley Party for the local elections, and got a councillor in and, indeed, put Charlton back in the Valley.

My other manifesto ideas were a cable car for pensioners to the top of Greenwich Hill (this has since been suggested successfully by the Millennium Committee), proper rides at funfairs and proper prizes, bringing real fog back to London for old times' sake, and concreting the Thames so people can travel about more easily.

I've always felt detached from politics because government represents authority, whether Labour or Conservative. When I was in prison, the strangest thing I noticed was that prisoners always had a better deal under a right-wing government. Parole was brought in by a Conservative government, and so was one-third and later half remission. I also used to think that, when a Conservative government was in power, the prison officers were happier and therefore the prisoners were treated better. Due to recent developments with the 'Hang 'Em and Flog 'Em' brigade, this is no longer the case.

After I came out of Grendon in the autumn of 1973, I met and lived with someone called Mazzie Merrick whose father was a big wheel at the Bank of England. Mazzie was a striking girl in the Marilyn Monroe mould and at the beginning of our relationship, just like any other, we were shagging like rabbits anytime, anywhere, anyhow. I bought her a lettuce for her birthday to see if she ate like a rabbit too. We moved into my grandmother's old flat and I tried 'proper' work – on an ice-cream van, although this wasn't much good in February – but frequent visitors included Dexie Doug Davies, Bernie from Birmingham and other criminal associates.

Mazzie and I were not destined to last. She got out while the going was bad. She was, and is, a lovely woman and now lives in the West Country with her husband and fourteen-year-old daughter.

I had come out of prison thinking I was going to go straight until I met someone I'd known at school who had become a postman. He started to sell me all the chequecards and chequebooks he could find in the mail. It's the ideal scenario – you can just go into any shop and buy anything. Which Bernie and I did. We bought literally *anything*, no matter how tacky. I got one of those awful lamps with the floating oil and bubbles, like in *The Prisoner*. Very sixties. And I bought loads of clothes which, of course, became somewhat unfashionable while I was doing another prison sentence.

After we left Grendon, Bernie and I grew beards. One day we were wandering round the West End, our pockets stuffed with other people's chequebooks and chequecards, when a policeman came up to us and said, 'I'm looking for two blokes with beards.'

I was worried. 'Oh, yeah?' I said.

'Yes,' he replied.

He wanted us for an identity parade and took us down to Vine Street police station where they had another character with a beard who'd been accused of cheque frauds. A shopkeeper came along the line and picked out Bernie by mistake. We were released, of course, because we were two 'innocent passers-by' co-operating fully with the Boys in Blue.

After a year of systematic crime, we were arrested in Torquay and I got three years for £57,000 of cheque fraud and fetched up back in Exeter prison, where I was almost put on patches again because I'd been a Category A prisoner before. Both Bernie and I were given 'vocational' tests. If you were the lowest of the low, you were put on a bricklayers' course, but if you were at the top, as I was, it was radio and television. I thought, Great! I'll get on telly!

But it turned out they meant fixing them.

Bernie was sent to Nottingham and I went to Lewes in Sussex, where I acquired the nickname Biggles. I still had the beard, because it was easier than shaving every day and asking permission for razors, and I took to playing football in the lunch breaks. One day people down the front were shouting: 'Oi! Goggles!' at the same time as someone at the back was yelling: 'Beardie!' The man who played alongside me got it mixed up and called me Biggles.

I used to play bridge with a fellow named Johnny Hart. He was great until he got depressed. He saw a psychiatrist who gave him some tablets, but then he became paranoid. When you play bridge with someone, you might say to them, 'You shouldn't have led with that card,' and they'll take it on board. After he started the tablets, if you said that to Johnny Hart he'd explode.

One day during dinner, all of a sudden, just in front of me, I saw Johnny Hart get up and stab a black guy. He'd helped

79

himself to a ten-inch knife from the kitchen and pushed it in this fellow's back, right up to the hilt. The black guy collapsed over my table. There was a long silence.

Then all the other black guys got up and chased Johnny.

When he went to court for attempted murder, we found out he'd done it because he thought his victim was wearing his plimsolls.

Some years later I read that Johnny Hart had burgled a house, tied a couple up and murdered the wife. Maybe it hadn't been the tablets and he was a psychopath after all.

Anyway, I passed the radio and television course – and A Levels in art and history of art plus English. Then I was transferred back to Exeter where I started work on the prison farm. Prison is the only form of education from which you can't be expelled. It's an education in itself.

While I was at Exeter a fellow con was a solicitor who had refused to pay his ex-wife maintenance. Instead, he would walk into his local police station every July, confess that he hadn't given her any money, go to the magistrates' court, where he was sentenced to six weeks in prison (reduced to four with remission), and spend four weeks' holiday on the farm. They used to save a place for him every year. When I arrived he'd been doing it for six or seven years.

I think working on the prison farm was that made me go straight, because I was in open conditions for about a year. I was treated decently too which had a *lot* to do with it. There was a civilian worker, Ron Parker, on the farm, who invited me round to his house every Sunday to have dinner with his family. He played a bit of jazz organ. I still see him. He lives in Cornwall now and I don't think he knows the effect he had on my life.

My going straight was a combination of being treated well and that I'd grown up: many ex-cons go straight when they're around thirty. I suppose it's just a maturing process. Most prisoners are under thirty – and that's in the jails that only have people over twenty-one.

For whatever reason, I decided to go straight, get out of prison and get into showbiz.

CHAPTER 5

THE GREATEST SHOW ON LEGS

I came out of Exeter three days after Jubilee Day in 1977. Unless you're young enough to be a footballer, there are only two things you can do when you come out of prison and you want immediate employment. You can either be a minicab driver or you can go into showbusiness. I did both.

Alan Curry – a friend of Wizo – who later joined the Greatest Show on Legs, had been looking for a flat and had found a vast Victorian pile in Micheldever Road in Lee Green, half a mile from Lewisham. A woman called Sally Niblett lived there. Her husband, a well-known doctor, was disabled but had taken himself, his wheelchair and their five boys off to Papua New Guinea leaving her alone in this massive house. So Alan moved in. He told Wizo about the house, Wizo told me and I moved in too. (At this point, Wizo was a lifeguard at a local swimming pool, although he couldn't swim – or, at least, not in the traditional sense.) Then my mate Martin Potter moved in and, over the years, Sally must have had seventy different tenants in that house. Even my sister lived there for a time. Nearly everyone I know has lived there.

The house next door was owned by a man called Michael, who was clinically mad. He used to cut the hedge in the morning, then stick the leaves back on with glue and Sellotape. The maddest goings-on in the world took place at Sally Niblett's house. There was a bloke called Vic, who thought he was practical but he wasn't. He kept a car engine he was repairing in his bedroom but it never worked. Once he tried to come into my room, but he hit his head on a wooden beam across the door. He ran downstairs, got a chainsaw, came back up and started to saw through the wood.

Dave was another of Sally's 'guests'. He bought an old taxi, took the body off it and decided to remake it in wood, because he was a bit of a chippie. After about two years, he decided to take his car for a test run. He came out of the drive, turned left and, after about a hundred yards, was stopped by the police, who said,

'You can't have this. It's illegal. You've got no MOT certificate.' He re-parked it in the drive where it stayed for fifteen years until it rotted away.

Sally eventually moved into the basement because so many people were living in her house. Everyone paid her five pounds a week for whichever room they had. It was the weirdest house you could ever imagine. It made the house in BBC TV's *The Young Ones* look like a palace. Once, I wanted to have a chicken-run in the garden so I bought two chickens and put them in the oven while I built the chicken-run. Sally came home and switched the oven on. She never noticed what was inside it. Another time, we moved a sofa from a house round the corner. We didn't have a van to put it in, so towed it behind my old Austin Cambridge car, with Vic sitting on the sofa as we drove round the streets – until I went round a corner sharpish. The rope snapped and Vic and the sofa hurtled straight into the Manor Lane Café.

It was while I was living at Micheldever Road that I became a minicab-driver. 'Alec the Greek', who wasn't a Greek, lent me sixty-five pounds to buy a four-door Renault 4 saloon. At about the same time, I saw a notice in the local paper,

---

WANTED FOR THEATRE
GROUP
ACTORS

---

and thought, I'll have a go at that!

This was the 1970s so being in a theatre group meant that somebody gave you a grant and you toured round scaring kids for an hour at a time. I went to the audition and they were all standing in a circle chanting, 'Taaaaall as a tree! Smaaaall as a mouse!' Then: 'Oooooooh! Eeeeeeeh!'

And I thought, What the fuck's going on here?

But I still reckoned I'd have a go at it.

I had a boxer dog with me – I was looking after him for someone – and as I tried doing *Taaaaall as a tree!* he was trying to shag my leg. Everyone was taking it seriously but, on the other side of the room, for a fellow called Martin Soan. He looked at me and he looked at the boxer, and I looked at him and we knew we were going to get on. We did.

I went minicabbing with the dog in the car. There was a girl in this theatre group who was very big. Well, let's be honest, she was fat. She fancied me. I don't know why, but she did.

I went to the minicab office one night around 1 a.m. and this girl was there, waiting for me. She said, 'Can you take me home to Peckham, Malcolm?'

'All right,' I said.

Just as she was getting in the car, the minicab boss shouted, 'Oi! I've got another fare for Peckham, round the corner! Can you take him?'

'Yes,' I said, 'no problem.'

I drove round to pick up the fare, who was on the fourteenth floor of a tower block. I went in. The lift didn't work so I ran up the stairs, knocked on the door and yelled, 'Anyone cab for Peckham?'

This bloke came to the door, a bit drunk, and said, 'Can you take five?'

'Well,' I said, 'I don't think I *can*. I've got a dog in the car.' I didn't mention the girl.

So he called out, 'Mavis! We like dogs, don't we?'

'Yeah,' she called back. 'We *love* dogs!'

After he said he'd pay double, I agreed to take them all. I

ran down the stairs and shouted to the girl, 'Get in the boot!'

Full credit to her, she did. The boot in my Renault was at the front. When the family came down I saw that, luckily, they were quite small people. I put three in the back, with the dog over their laps, and the man and his wife in the front. Then I started up the engine. The fat girl must have panicked because the boot lid came slowly up and her face rose in front of the windscreen. The man asked the not unreasonable question, 'Who's that?'

'Dunno,' I said.

The lid of the boot went down and we drove off to Peckham. He never mentioned it again. Nor did I.

When I first met him, Martin Soan had a Punch and Judy show called The Greatest Show on Legs. In a normal Punch and Judy show, the booth stands on the ground but Martin had decided to strap it on the top half of his body so that his legs stuck out beneath. It was a good idea because, if the show went badly, he could just run away with the whole thing attached to him.

He was about twenty-three at the time and he had a young lad called Tom helping him. Tom had to stand out at the front as the 'interpreter' and 'bottler'. The interpreter articulates to the audience Punch's squawkings; the bottler goes round with the hat collecting money. In olden days, they took a bottle which contained a live fly; the bottler had to keep his thumb over the top unless people were putting money in. If the fly wasn't in the bottle when he handed it over, the performer knew his helper had been nicking money out of it. Martin suggested I should take over as his interpreter and bottler.

Our first show was in the winter of 1978. We performed to kids at the Riverdale Centre in Lewisham and I was nervous. I don't get nervous now, but I've never been happy working in front of kids: they pick out your faults straightaway. The next show we played was outside a pub called the Cutty Sark by the Thames. Sometimes Martin used to do a bit of fire-eating. This time he decided to bend down and blow the fire between his legs. He was starting to do this when a toddler ran towards him just as he blew out a huge ball of flame, which missed the child by inches. The kid started screaming and all the parents complained.

When we did the Punch and Judy show at the Deptford Festival (a misnomer in itself), we went down quite well. A man came up to us with Marcel Steiner of the Smallest Theatre in the World – which is a theatre built on an ordinary motorcycle – and put a fiver in our hat, the equivalent then of giving a busker fifty pounds today.

'Do you know who that was?' Martin said to me. 'That was Neil Innes from the Bonzo Dog Doo Dah Band.' And then I recognised him, from when I'd played harmonica with the Bonzos in South East London pubs. He, of course, hadn't recognised me.

We carried on doing the kids' shows for a while but it wasn't really our sort of thing. Eventually I suggested, 'Why don't we just get in the van and go round doing a Punch and Judy show for adults? A bit of swearing and all sorts.'

We recruited Barry Sherlock, my childhood chum, as the banjo player, and we invited Alan Curry to join us because he had a van. We started in Brighton, did a couple of shows in the shopping precinct, and Barry did his normal trick and gave it all up – as he's done with many other things, including playing with Squeeze and Kate Bush. At the first sign of success he'd be off. Alan took over Barry's role and we went down to Devon where we had some good times.

Much later, Janet Street-Porter said, 'Comedy is The New Rock 'n' Roll' and, when you have the likes of Rob Newman and David Baddiel playing Wembley, it's arguably true. The Greatest Show on Legs playing Devon wasn't quite on the same scale. We were more like medieval troubadours, travelling round from place to place. When we first toured, we didn't stay in hotels. I used to say to the audience, 'We haven't got anywhere to stay tonight.

THE GREATEST SHOW ON LEGS

Can anybody put us up?' And 99 per cent of the time someone did. Normally female. Women put us up, put up with us and we put it up them – one of the attractions of touring.

I think the comedian Tony Allen is usually credited with coining the phrase 'Alternative Cabaret'. But in 1978, years before the Comedy Store, the local yacht club at Salcombe in Devon was putting on mainstream acts and the landlord at the nearby Ferry Inn put a notice in the local paper advertising,

---

ALTERNATIVE CABARET

AT THE FERRY INN

---

meaning an 'alternative' to the yacht club's cabaret. *That* was the first time the phrase was used, as far as I know.

The Ferry Inn has a patio by the river estuary. Normally when we performed we left out a hat for the audience to throw money in but the first time we played there, I said to Martin, 'What you should do is, at the end of the show, unstrap the booth from yourself, dive over the wall into the sea, swim round to the steps, come up, then go round with the hat. They'll love it.'

So he did. Performed. Whoosh! Over the wall. Into the sea. Round with the hat. Thirty quid in our pockets.

The next day we went back to do the show again. He unstrapped the booth. Whoosh! Over the wall. We saw him leap over, there was a scream, a silence, and he came up the steps covered in seaweed and blood. The tide had gone out. I told him to go round with the hat anyway but we only got two pounds.

The reason we went to the West Country was that I knew it from my criminal days and I loved the area. When we got there, though, we discovered all these summer fairs and even more life than in London. We had found our niche. There was a Festival of Fools, a Hood Fair, and lots of arty types and hippies. But we were seen as rather 'base' because we were doing Punch and Judy. And I had little in common with these people because I was still wearing my mohair suit. There were lots of theatre groups doing 'warm-ups'. (The Greatest Show on Legs used to do sober-ups.) Somehow, though, apart from the radical feminists, audiences liked us. The feminists disapproved of our generally coarse attitude and went for the more arty, drifty type. The adult Punch and Judy show upset them. Back in those days, if you mentioned the words 'knob' and 'cunt', that was it. Chris Lynam, another fine performer of the weird school, had an act involving a huge rubber penis about five feet long and a foot wide. At the end of his act, he flapped it on to a table and pissed out of it. That part of the act was banned from Devon. There was a feminist group called Cunning Stunts, but that was OK because they were women and they'd all been to Dartington, the liberal college for the arts in Totnes. Ironically they all got off with the most sexist men imaginable, which is often the way with feminists. I should know, I've shagged loads of 'em – but I'm not as horribly macho as some of the men feminists go for. I think if you get women laughing you're half-way there.

We went to East Anglia too. In Norfolk, there were 'tree fairs' like the one at Rougham, where you could see cabaret and theatre groups. They were run by a woman called Tarbie, who lived in an amazing Norfolk cottage, and were mostly on a smaller scale than the West Country fairs.

When we were down in the South West, we did fairs at the weekend but midweek went to the roughest pub in the area. The Queen Vic in Exeter was always full of Hell's Angels and people who recognised me from when I'd been in Exeter prison four or five years previously. But they were a fantastic audience. We were doing a Punch and Judy show and grown men were shouting: 'That's the way to do it! Behind you!'

It probably helped that there was masturbation, sex and a punk rocker in it.

I decided to try for some television publicity for the show. The local ITV station was then Westward Television and I phoned the producer on *Westward Diary*, their local news magazine programme. 'Hello,' I said. 'We're doing a Punch and Judy show in your area. Very witty. Everyone loves it. Can we go on *Westward Diary*?'

'No!' he said.

So when I came out of the phone box, Martin asked, 'How did you get on?'

'We're on tomorrow night,' I said.

We went all the way down to Plymouth and I was too embarrassed to tell them he'd said No. I hate failure. When we got to the TV studios, I said to the receptionist, 'Hello. We're the Greatest Show on Legs. We're on *Westward Diary* tonight.'

She rang upstairs and the producer had gone to London for the day. But he'd written down 'The Greatest Show on Legs' on a bit of paper, so she said, 'Yes. That's right. You *are* on.'

And we were. We appeared on *Westward Diary* and, at the end, someone came running over and asked me, 'Are you in Equity?'

'Yes,' I said, quick as a flash.

She gave me an Equity contract for £180. I sent it to the union and was accepted into it. People used to go to drama school and sweep floors to get an Equity card. Silly buggers.

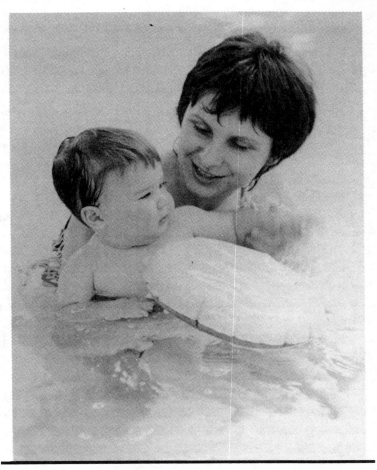

CHAPTER 6

PERCY THE PEACOCK FELL OUT OF THE TREE

Back in South East London after our Alternative Summer
Season, I met Pip, the woman with whom I was to spend the next
thirteen years. She was at my local pub, the Crown, in Blackheath.
I chatted up two girls and fancied the tarty-looking one, but I
ended up with the feminist, who was Pip. In long-term relationships, I tend to go for a woman who's straight and strong. Otherwise, perhaps, I'd go completely off the rails and be in some gutter
injecting heroin.

Most of my partners have been intelligent and have worked
in the caring professions, teachers, nurses, etc. Pip is a strong
woman and so is my wife, Jane, both emotionally and intellectually.
I've had relationships outside steady ones with more bimbo-ish
types. When I was living with Pip I went off with a stripper. She
had been featured in the *Penthouse* centrefold, and was the epit-
ome of a glamorous woman, but she wasn't very bright and didn't
last long.

For a long-term relationship, intelligence is important,
because you've got to be able to talk to each other after the three
hours of sexual activity. The 'Malcolm Hardee' stage character
wouldn't be interested in a clever woman, but that's just an exag-
gerated persona I use to link up with a lot of the men in the
audience. It's a 'Cor! Look at her!' thing, which all men do. I've
seen Ben Elton do it.

At the time I met Pip, I was still alternating the Greatest Show
on Legs with minicabbing until, after about two years of being
straight, I was arrested in 1978 for a burglary I didn't commit.
I'd been helping John McNulty, whom I'd known briefly in Lewes
prison. He had five days' home leave and I felt sorry for him. I
let him stay a night at the house in Micheldever Road and, for the
five days, I drove him in my minicab wherever he wanted to go
without charging him.

When he returned to prison, I read an article in the *Evening*

Standard, which said that the police were looking for a hooded rapist and burglar who had been operating in the South East London area. I realised that this character had been active during McNulty's five-day home leave and decided to tell the police about my suspicions. After they had questioned him, the police brought me in and wanted to keep hold of me because they needed me to testify against him, to say I'd picked him up from these various spots, which I had, though I hadn't known what he was doing. Luckily I'd never picked him up from any spot where he'd commit-. ted a rape, only burglaries. I was charged with burglary and stealing a key worth seventy-five pence: all he'd stolen on one burglary I'd picked him up from was the key out of the side door. I got two years and went to Ford open prison.

Ford was quite a nice place. The footballer George Best had done time there as had the England football captain Tony Adams. I always tell people I played in the same football team as George Best and Tony Adams, although, tragically, not at the same time. While I was away, the Greatest Show on Legs was joined by a fellow nicknamed 'Knob Rot', I've no idea why. He didn't last long, but Martin and Alan carried on through that summer. In 1979, after nine months, I was released on appeal and went back to Micheldever Road, where Pip had set up a home of sorts for us in one of the rooms. I started living with her although I didn't really want to live with anyone. I lived with Pip *slightly* by mistake but we got on all right and I even went to visit her parents, who are extremely upper-middle class. Pip's full name is Philippa and I couldn't call her Pip in their house. Her mother's a magistrate and her father has his own business and is in the local Rotary Club. They hated me on sight and after we got home Pip had a letter asking, 'Who was that dreadful man you brought with you?'

Pip's parents never really liked me – but I was still invited over to their place every other Christmas. They had silver napkin

95

rings with their names on. I never got my name on one, though. It's a bit better since we split up because I think they dislike the new boyfriend even more than they did me. He's a gardener but very hippie-ish . . .

When I came out of Ford, I showed Martin some sketches I'd written there because I was fed up with the Punch and Judy show. One included the famous speech from *Henry V*, 'Once more unto the breach dear friends . . .' My mum got hold of a Shakespearian-type costume with a lion on the front, which I wore, and we did the old music-hall thing in which I stood at the front, delivered the speech with my arms held behind me and Martin at my back, his arms coming underneath my armpits so they looked as if they were mine. I also wore a crown. We had a New Zealander roadie called Scott and I used the crown as part of an old joke. I needed his help on that. ' "A horse! A horse!" ' I would say. ' "My kingdom for a horse!" '

Then Scott as the audience plant stood up holding a newspaper and said: ' 'Ere, mate, I've got an 'orse . . . Sonny Boy in the two-thirty at Kempton Park!'

I would take off my crown, tear it in half and say: 'All right! I'll have half a crown each way.' Money had gone decimal ten years before, but the joke still worked, even though Scott, one of the biggest, toughest blokes you could meet, got stage fright. He went all red and squeaked out his words like a chipmunk.

While all this was going on, I was still living with Pip. She was a probation officer when I met her – not *my* probation officer – but decided to do a postgraduate degree at the University of Kent in Canterbury, so we had to find somewhere betwixt Canterbury and London, where most of my work was. Eventually, we discovered a mansion near Maidstone in Kent where we were offered a free flat in exchange for twelve hours' gardening and twelve hours' housework a week. We got it through a Maidstone-based friend of mine, Terry Lovell, who had seen an advert in the local paper. The house was owned by a wealthy Scotsman, who worked for the Bank of America and who, of course, required me to supply a reference. I asked Terry to write one. As a joke he did two: one glowing testimonial informing the Scotsman of my gardening skills, and one derogatory but truthful statement describing my prison record and general unreliability. He intended to send me the bad one and make out it was a copy of the reference he had sent the Scotsman. Unfortunately, he got the envelopes mixed up.

When the Scotsman got the bad but truthful version, he reckoned it was so far-fetched it must be a joke, so Pip and I got the flat anyway.

I turned out to be anything but an expert gardener. I pulled up the wife's asparagus plants which didn't go down very well as they take five years to produce anything and were already in their fourth year. In the end, my supposed twelve hours of gardening involved inviting six friends down for the weekend and each had to do two hours. We got someone else in to do the housework for thirty pounds a week, referred to that as 'rent' and Pip claimed it back from her student grant.

The Scotsman and his family also had a couple of ponies, some peacocks, a white rabbit, three dogs and about a million bloody guinea pigs. The guinea pigs died regularly and Percy the Peacock twice froze and fell out of his tree that winter. He recovered – the first time.

There were three kids: a son, who went to boarding school, and two daughters, who were at the local comprehensive. One of the girls was the owner of the white rabbit, which was called Snowy. Sadly, one of the dogs got hold of Snowy and killed him. The woman had recently become vegetarian and asked me to bury him for them, which I did. Then I was told that I had to break the news of his death to his unwitting owner. After some thought, I said to both girls, 'Those of you who think you've got a white rabbit called Snowy, one step forward.' The ex-rabbit fancier did as she was asked and I said, 'Where do you think you're going?'

She was a bit upset, but later they invited Pip and me down for dinner that evening. We were all sitting round the table when the dog trotted in with something hanging out of its mouth, which it plonked beside her. Snowy. I hadn't buried him deep enough. A few more tears were shed.

On New Year's Eve, the family went to Scotland and I was left in charge of the whole lot – animals and all. One of the ponies was very stubborn. In the morning, I had to lead him round the family's croquet lawn into the field where he spent the day, then back to the stable at night. Unfortunately, we'd had our own New Year's Eve party with Dave 'Bagpipe' Brooks, Dave the Druid and about a hundred other lunatic friends. It had been a bit of a wild night.

The next morning, I had to get up to let the pony out, which promptly decided to bolt. I hung on to its tail to stop it getting away – and succeeded – but the croquet lawn was another story. Where before there had been a flat expanse of flawless green, there were now neat furrows, made by my boots right across it, where I'd been dragged water-ski style, and any number of hoofprints. The family were coming back the next day. It was Nightmare Manor. I had to get all the party guests to work on restoring the lawn to its original pristine condition. When they got back the family didn't notice anything amiss.

I had met Dave the Druid, also known as Digger Dave, in Exeter prison. He was into mysticism, but he was always up to some scam too. He lived, like everybody else, in Micheldever Road. He performed briefly with the Greatest Show on Legs, then moved to Truro in Cornwall, and made 'Roman' masks. He said he'd got them out of the sea and that they were the real thing, but he had a mould. He didn't share the Greatest Show on Legs's idea of comedy. He was more the morris-dancing sort: he liked bells and bladders on the ends of sticks.

We left the mansion when Pip's university course ended and we moved back to London. I'd been spending a lot of time in London anyway – Maidstone was only thirty minutes' drive away. Unknown to Pip, I'd been having an affair with a woman called Mandy Moy, the daughter of a Greenwich businessman. He owned a house called the Man in the Moon, an ex-pub which had become a shop, and Pip and I moved into the top storey. The Greenwich meridian line went straight through the building, so when we lived there I was able to eat my dinner in the Western Hemisphere and eject it in my toilet in the Eastern Hemisphere.

Mandy had three eccentric brothers, Toby, Jeremy and Rupert. Toby has a place called the Junk Shop in Greenwich and walks around barefoot. Recently, I bought a joke-box off him – it's like a juke-box except it tells jokes instead of playing records. He came to my club Up the Creek to get the money but when my business partners saw him they thought he was a crustie or a tramp and wouldn't give it to him. Yet he's the son of one of the richest men in Greenwich.

Mandy looked fairly normal. She was and is a nurse at Greenwich hospital. She refused to be supported by her father and went her own way. She still does.

By January 1980, three of us were performing regularly in the Greatest Show on Legs – Martin, me and Christian Steiner, son of Marcel who ran the Smallest Theatre in the World. We'd stopped doing Punch and Judy shows and were now doing sketch-based stuff. There was a big article on us in the London *Evening News*, in which Val Hennessey called us 'cult figures'. I immediately got my ear pierced.

We did lots of shows at Camden Lock because we had persuaded Greater London Arts to give us a grant to perform there. Once I saw John Cleese watching us from the restaurant and later I noticed him doing some of our sketches on *The Secret Policeman's Ball*, such as the Shakespeare-without-arms. We had just started doing our nude Balloon Dance, but with bits of paper instead of balloons, and he did the same routine with clothes on which, of course, is only half as funny.

When Christian and Martin fell out, we recruited a bloke called Pete, who played guitar and could make up a song instantly in any style. At the end of the shows we collected money in a hat. Naturally a large proportion was spent on booze. Pete was a bit put out by this, because he didn't drink, and left us.

Dave Brooks, the jazz bagpipe player who wasn't Scottish, took his place. He came from Hampstead, but he was excellent on the pipes. Our problem was that he insisted he couldn't tune up outside: he had to do it where we were going to perform because of temperature changes and other such technical issues. Thus the first section of the Greatest Show on Legs's act consisted of Dave tuning up. This probably took two minutes but seemed like an hour. Then he'd play a number – in tune – after which Martin and I would burst on. If he went down well, though, Dave would do another number and, if that went well, another and so on and . . . Sometimes he'd do about thirty minutes of piping in what was meant to be a forty-five minute show.

We also performed at a Woolwich club called the Tramshed. There we were known as the New Fundation and joined forces with Rik Mayall and Ade Edmondson, who had a double-act called 20th Century Coyote. The *old* Fundation had been Hale & Pace, Joe Griffiths and Phil Skinner, who did a different set there every week. It was a middle-of-the-road variety show, but good. I didn't know any of this. I'd only been out of prison two weeks when we first played there. The new manager at the Tramshed had chucked out the old Fundation because he thought they were too low-brow. We did our Punch and Judy show with a few sketches and, after our first performance, he said: 'Very good. Can you come back next week and do a different show?' which threw me, because I had expected to do the same Punch and Judy show every week.

One of the new routines we worked out for the Tramshed was 'Mongo the Strongman'. Martin wore a leotard, which also covered his arms and part of his legs. Under this, where muscles would be, he put deflated balloons connected to a series of rubber tubes, which came out of the neck of the leotard; he draped himself with a veil, like some Arab woman from a harem, to hide the tubes. When he flexed his muscles, he blew up the balloons via the tubes. Very Popeye. Out the front I played the part of a traditional circus barker.

Part of the Mongo routine involved Martin lying down and me putting a paving slab on his chest, a brick on the paving slab and, the *pièce de résistance*, an egg on the brick. Then I had to hit the egg with a ten-pound sledgehammer. The brick split. It looked like Martin was taking a lot of weight but the size of the paving slab absorbed the pressure and – theoretically – didn't hurt. When we did it at the Tramshed, however, I was somewhat the worse for the demon drink.

During the act, I'd been using a silver-topped walking cane, with which I'd accidentally hit him in the testicles. By the time I'd put the paving slab, brick and egg on his chest and picked up the sledgehammer I could see he was a bit worried. He was in agony, but the audience liked it.

'Mongo the Strongman' was followed by 'Sidney the Sea-lion'. For this, Martin – he always does the hard work – had to get the bottom half of his body into the inner tube of a truck tyre. He also wore a clown's red nose painted black and whiskers on his upper lip and cheeks. He came on stage like that, waddling like a sea-lion up to a horn fitted with a rubber ball at the end – like Harpo Marx's – pressed it and went oink-oink. I used to ask him questions, one oink for yes, two for no. We tried it several times, but it never worked properly because the inner tube kept coming off. Good idea of Martin's, though. We experimented quite a lot.

During any Greatest Show on Legs performance, we needed a theatrical backdrop, to change behind, to drink behind and to

101

hide the bucket for pissing in. Once, I decided we'd have three doors at the back of the stage. They were built so that they could open inwards, outwards, left to right or right to left or spin on their axis either horizontally or vertically. It was a technical nightmare, but the idea was that every time someone came on stage, he would enter through a different door in a different way. For the finale, we were going to come in with the doors swinging over from top to bottom. I managed all right but Martin, as usual, overdid it. He spun round and round on his door, then fell flat on his face. Blood poured from his nose and that was the end of the show. The audience, of course, loved it. We gave up on the doors there and then, not just because they were hideously complicated but because they were so heavy and we didn't have a van big enough to put them in. Martin used the idea again, but with just one door, in comedian Boothby Graffoe's successful 1995 Edinburgh Fringe show.

The original doors were burnt in a fire on Chris Lynam's double-decker bus. We used to store our props on it, but he kept it in South East London where, Peckham being Peckham, the bus was the target of an arson attack.

The Tramshed was good training for the six weeks we did it because we learnt to write a-show-a-week in an hour: myself, Martin, Rik Mayall and Ade Edmondson. During those six weeks, Rik mentioned a new venue in the West End called the Comedy Store.

It was the first proper alternative comedy venue in Central London and I will always regret missing the first week, but I was there nearly every week after that with the Greatest Show on Legs. The original Comedy Store had a gong. You got up on stage and if you survived three shows without getting gonged off, you were on the payroll. Few made it but we did. Rik Mayall and Ade Edmondson did. Pete Richardson (now owner of the Comic Strip) did. Nigel Planer did. Tony Allen always survived and so did Keith

Allen: if he hadn't, he would probably have torn the gong off the wall. In early 1980, we became a regular team there.

At the time, the Comedy Store was in a building that housed an old strip club called the Gargoyle, just off Dean Street. It was confusing for some. Japanese tourists used to come into the Comedy Store thinking they were going to see a strip show – sometimes they *did* see one when the Greatest Show on Legs were performing. Other times the trendy, politically correct comedy audience went into the strip club by mistake, which was even funnier. Pete Rosengard, who ran the Comedy Store, was a shrewd character. He later managed a pop group called Curiosity Killed the Cat and has never given up his 'day job' as top salesman for Abbey Life Insurance. He had been to the States, had seen how the Los Angeles Comedy Store worked, and had approached Don Ward, the owner of this Soho club. (He now owns the current Comedy Store outright.) This was in 1980, when the Thatcher years were just kicking in. On the one hand, there were mainstream frilly shirt and dinner-jacket comics telling mother-in-law and racist jokes – they got booed off, because the audience were champagne socialists – and on the other hand, you had political comics.

When we were on the payroll, we got fifteen pounds a night between three of us from the Comedy Store. Tony Allen started as the main compère while we were there, until, after about six weeks, Alexei Sayle took over.

By the summer of 1981, we were also appearing nightly in a West End stage show. One of the producers had decided to get together all the eccentric acts he could find and put them in one show. He called it *The Mad Show* and put it on at the Collegiate (now the Bloomsbury) Theatre. It was a good idea, but his only previous showbiz experience had been writing a play called *Noddy the Squaddie* when he was at Sandhurst Military College. It had been performed to the upper echelons of the Army and he said it had been highly satirical but . . .

He and his partner poured vast sums of money into one of these speciality acts by building a 5,700-gallon tank on the stage, putting a weighted-down piano in it and filling the tank with water. Then one Ronnie Smith would come on stage, wearing flippers, and sing 'Flip! Flop! Splish! Splash!'. His finale was to climb up a ladder, get in the tank, swim down to the piano, wearing sub-aqua gear, and play it. Except that he didn't play. You can't play a piano under-water. He mimed, painfully obviously, to a tape. Even if there had been any applause, he wouldn't have heard it underwater.

Another *Mad Show* act, J. J. Waller lay on a bed of nails. This would take a normal human being three or four minutes but he could extend it into a half-hour performance. He wore a tight leopardskin costume and was very thin. He used to hold up the bed of nails and say: 'Will you, sir, hold *this* potato?' and throw a potato into the audience. Then he'd hurl a few more potatoes at the audience and get them to throw them at the bed of nails where they stuck. He ended his act by getting someone to stand on his stomach while he lay on the bed of nails. Lying on a bed of nails doesn't hurt – provided the nails are close to each other.

Also on *The Mad Show* was Chris Luby, who did aeroplane impressions. More about him later. Remember the name.

Anthony Irvine did an act in which he crawled across the stage wearing a yellow sou'wester, cape and wellington boots, got up a ladder, then put a chain with a hook on it between the two parts of the stepladder and picked up a bag. He took a toothbrush out of the bag, cleaned his teeth, got down the steps and crawled off stage. This took between ten and twenty minutes depending on audience response. Today he calls himself the Iceman and melts a block of ice on stage. That's his act. At the 1995 Edinburgh Fringe he jointly won the Tapwater Award for Most Bizarre Act with Charlie Chuck and me.

Bob Flag was also in *The Mad Show* with an act involving a saxophone. He came on stage several times dressed in various

Army regalia. It seems worth mentioning that his face was used in the film of Orwell's *1984* as Big Brother.

There was Norman Milligan, too, who wore an American Army uniform and a metal helmet like General Patton's on his top half with stockings and suspenders below. He sang a rambling monologue about the war.

The Greatest Show on Legs did the Balloon Dance. At the time, there was a play on called *The Romans in Britain*, in which men pranced around nude on stage. Mary Whitehouse objected to it. About a week later, I read that she liked cha-cha music. I thought, I know what to do. We'll do a sketch and be naked in it but we'll have cha-cha music and then everybody will be happy. So we ended up with the Balloon Dance. All three of us, stark naked except for socks, did the cha-cha while holding two balloons each and swapping them round on the fourth beat to cover our genitals. That's it. It was popular with audiences. Lovely. We also tap-danced with dustbin lids on our feet, and we did a Scottish sword-dance using members of the audience instead of swords.

The Mad Show didn't bring in big audiences so, in a rare canny moment, the producers did a deal with Japanese television to get their money back. They put on a 'Mr Looniverse' competition to find the most eccentric acts in the world, which eventually consisted of the cast of *The Mad Show* and some imported Japanese acts, one of which played musical vegetables. He hollowed out carrots and suchlike, then blew through them. He couldn't speak much English and foolishly asked us to translate the names of the vegetables.

When he picked up a marrow, we told him, 'Tomato.' A carrot: 'Goldfish.' A cucumber: 'Tractor.' And so on. Then he went on stage with his wheelbarrow full of vegetables, picked up a cucumber and said, 'Tlactah!'

We were almost hoist by our own petard. The audience thought he was taking the piss and he nearly won.

Another Japanese act was 'The Monkey Man', who went round the stage like a monkey. He was quite agile but the point of it escaped me.

We won the competition and got £1000 from the Japanese. We had to do our tap-dancing-with-dustbin-lids routine, because they couldn't show the Balloon Dance on Japanese TV. Too naughty.

That was the peak of *The Mad Show*. After about eight weeks, one of the producers called the cast together and said, 'Well, I'm afraid we're not going to be able to pay you for ten weeks.' The orchestra immediately got up and walked out the door.

In the final days, people were dismantling the hired props on stage as the show was going on. On the last night, the water tank was still there so the Greatest Show on Legs, ever keen on a dip, plunged in and swam around while Ronnie Smith mimed playing the piano.

But *The Mad Show* had been a success for us in that it led to our Big Break. We were seen by Chris Tarrant, who was preparing his upcoming Central TV series *OTT*, and also by the researchers for LWT's upcoming series *Game for a Laugh*.

As well as *The Mad Show* we were also doing the Tramshed and the Comedy Store and we were also still performing at hippie fairs in Norfolk and the West Country – which is where we met the Box Brothers, a four-piece swing band. I arranged a tour of Holland featuring the Greatest Show on Legs and the Box Brothers.

When we got to the border, the Dutch customs officials took almost all our money. At that time, if you went into Holland with electronic equipment, you had to hand over enough money to cover the cost of the equipment as a guarantee that you wouldn't sell it within the country. (It was returned to you when you left Holland with the same equipment.) Fair enough. But they took almost every penny we had. We had just enough petrol to get to the first gig.

The first day of that tour was the only show I've ever done completely sober. When we got to the theatre, the manager gave me sixty tickets with the word CONSUMPTIE printed on them but it wasn't until afterwards that I realised each ticket entitled us to a free drink – and that Dutch beer is strong.

We were popular in Holland and appeared at the annual Festival of Fools, which was held in Amsterdam one year and somewhere in England the next. In Amsterdam, a place called the Melkweg used to encourage performance art and British acts until, about 1984, they decided to go solely for Dutch acts, who were often appalling. I think the Melkweg has now become an acid house rave venue.

When we came back to England, we tried to make a point of appearing at the Comedy Store every week. If we were doing a gig ·in Manchester that finished at ten p.m., we would get straight on the train and arrive at the Comedy Store for last knockings at about one-thirty. We loved performing there. It was like a drug.

There were now two alternative comedy venues. Pete Richardson had split off from the Comedy Store and founded the Comic Strip at a place called the Boulevard Theatre, next door to Raymond's Revue Bar in Soho. We stuck with the Comedy Store.

We devised a Boy Scout routine, at the end of which Martin did a striptease, but we didn't have any Scout uniforms. My cousin Geoffrey, though, was a scoutmaster. He's educated and he's worked in a bank and he's never nicked a car, no shop-lifting, nothing. He's the black sheep of the family. I went round to see him and said, 'Hey, Geoffrey, can we borrow some Scout uniforms?'

'Well,' he said, 'you're not going to poke fun at the Scouts, are you?'

'Of course not,' I said. I thought it unwise to mention the striptease.

'All we're going to do,' I said, 'is have a little electric fire and sit round it and sing "Ging-gang-goolie-goolie" and the audience will love it.'

Cousin Geoffrey lent us the uniforms and, once again, I was making money from being a Scout.

A few weeks later we were doing a gig at the Tramshed, near to where Geoffrey lived, but I didn't tell him because I didn't want him to come along. At the end of the routine, Martin as usual did his striptease. Unfortunately, some pensioners were in the audience and so was the local paper's reporter. The pensioners complained to the reporter and, in Geoffrey's local paper, the following headline appeared: BOY SCOUT STRIPTEASE UPSETS PENSIONERS. There was a big picture of Martin with his socks off and me wearing the Scout uniform, complete with visible Scout troop logo. Geoffrey hasn't spoken to me since.

At the Comedy Store, we were a bit frowned on because we weren't cerebral – we did variety and music-hall sketches. Yet we often went down as well as, or better than, cerebral comics like Ben Elton or Pete Richardson because – I don't know – we had some *spunk*. We had a sense of irony. A bit like Spike Milligan, who was eventually accepted by his peers despite his lowly origins as Gunner Milligan from Brockley, a working-class area in South East London.

There was a university clique at the Comedy Store and the Comic Strip, but not Oxbridge-based. Rik Mayall, Ade Edmondson and Ben Elton had all been to Manchester and were from wealthy backgrounds. I'd met Pete Richardson five or six years before when I was in the West Country with Martin and we had performed our Punch and Judy show to some Swedish drama students in Pete's mum's house on Dartmoor. She was very well-heeled – swimming pool in the garden and all that sort of thing – and used to hire out the barn as a drama school for foreigners. The next time I saw Pete, he was playing the working-class wide-boy down the Comedy Store, as if he was from Sarf East London. Ben Elton *is* from South East London, but his uncle's Lord Elton and he's very well connected. Alexei Sayle told me about Ben's background. Alexei wasn't a university type. He was the son of a Liverpool train driver and had experience in community theatre. I remember seeing a poster of him playing in Bertolt Brecht's *The Threepenny Opera*. We appeared with him a lot at the Comedy Store. Martin and I used to do the *Henry V* sketch there almost every week. He once introduced us: 'Oh, well, here they are. They're just a couple of college kids.' I felt this was over-stating my prison A Levels and Martin's three weeks at art school.

He didn't like us, I think, because we weren't doing straight stand-up comedy at a microphone. I think he felt we were like drama students and not real comedians.

I recommended Alexei to the Albany Empire in Deptford. He got eight pounds and died a death. He was too odd for them: they were into politically correct comedy, Marcel Steiner and the Smallest Theatre in the World and they liked strong political theatre rather than what Alexei was doing, which was wearing a pork-pie hat and saying 'wanker' and 'cunt'. His breakthrough was BBC TV's *The Young Ones* with Rik and Ade.

The Greatest Show on Legs's breakthrough was doing the Balloon Dance on television. Dave 'Bagpipes' Brooks was supposed to be with the Greatest Show on Legs on the *OTT* pilot, but he'd buggered off to Cornwall – he'd had enough – right in the middle of *The Mad Show*. At about six-thirty one morning, I knocked up Martin Potter, who used to operate our tapes, and he came out with us and did the pilot for *OTT* and the audition for *Game for a Laugh*. We needed someone permanent, but Martin wasn't interested, so we conscripted Martin Clarke from Brighton, who'd been in a theatre group called Cliffhanger. He had a posh voice and looked a bit like Tony Blackburn, so we called him 'Sir Ralph'.

We had been invited to do the Balloon Dance on *Game for a Laugh* but, when we got to the LWT studios, the producer wouldn't let us do it naked. He said the show was for family viewing. 'But that's how we do it,' I said. 'That's the whole humour of it.'

He sent researchers out to get smaller and smaller items of underwear – even going into sex shops to get us jockstraps. But we held out and said, 'We're not doing it with pants on,' partly because we knew that *OTT* also wanted us in a month's time and they *would* let us do it naked. In the end, we did the Scottish sword dance on *Game for a Laugh*. We used the show's co-presenter Matthew Kelly as the cross swords. He had a broken leg at the time so although we kept our clothes on we still terrorised Matthew Kelly.

A month later, in January 1981, we finally got naked on TV when we did the Balloon Dance on *OTT*. It was one of the first programmes made by Central, who had taken over from ATV as the Birmingham ITV station. *OTT* was meant to be the all new, very daring adult version of Chris Tarrant's anarchic children's show *Tiswas*. Alexei Sayle performed on it every week and no one understood his humour. Lenny Henry, Bob Carolgees and Helen Atkinson-Wood were the other *OTT* regulars. On the first night we were there, the studio audience hadn't reacted well until we came on. We set the place alight – figuratively speaking. Afterwards there was a furore in the press and Mary Whitehouse complained, which is always a good thing.

We got on well with Chris Tarrant but, two or three years later, we did the Balloon Dance on another late-night TV series he had created. He was desperate for ratings, because they hadn't been very good, and got us in to do the last show. Afterwards, there was a big end-of-series party to which we weren't invited. Our roadie saw a jeroboam of champagne and nicked it. We were giving Helen Atkinson-Wood a lift back to London and were climbing into our Luton Transit when Chris Tarrant came running out, shouting, 'You've had my champagne!'

110

'No, we haven't!' I lied.

'You have!' he yelled. 'You'll never work on TV again!'

At this, Helen Atkinson-Wood jumped out of the van because she no longer wanted to be associated with us and the roadie drove us back to London.

I have heard since that Chris Tarrant says this incident involved the pub having some cutlery nicked, which had sentimental value to the landlord. That certainly wasn't us; we had just the one bottle of champagne.

Our first appearance on *OTT* turned out to be our big breakthrough and afterwards it was all congratulations. We ended up with an agent, Louis Parker, who treated us like the Chippendales. We went mainstream. We were doing hen nights and end-of-the-pier variety shows for two or three years – at Colwyn Bay and Blackpool, those sort of places. We were a novelty act doing a fifteen–twenty minute show for what was then an enormous amount of money: £500–£600 a night. But three of us had to share that with the roadie.

While we were thus engaged, Rik and Ade went on to TV success in *The Young Ones*. Pete Richardson was meant to have been in it too but he was replaced by someone recruited from a casting agency. *The Young Ones* garnered all the credit for being clever comedians, while our success was short-term, low-brow and mainstream. We even performed at a TUC conference in Blackpool where Neil Innes of the Bonzo Dogs (he still didn't recognise me) got booed off for being sexist: he was singing a song about a woman with tits and they didn't like him. But they liked the Greatest Show on Legs naked with balloons. Except that we didn't use balloons. No. We used photos of Mrs Thatcher to cover our bits, and when we turned round, it was to reveal our penises sticking out of her mouth. They loved it.

Chapter 7

Freddie Mercury, Glenda Jackson, Emma Thompson and a Tractor

As a result of the publicity over *OTT*, we were invited to perform at Freddie Mercury's fortieth birthday party. He was then one of the biggest international pop stars. We went to Club Xenon in Piccadilly, London, and were in a dressing room the size of a large cupboard with another twelve acts. A Russian acrobat went on first, then a midget, then a mime act and then us.

There was a high window in the door of our dressing room and we had to hold up the midget to find out what was happening in the main club, because the organisers wouldn't let us come out of the dressing room to see all the famous people: Freddie Mercury, Elton John, Rod Stewart, Princess Margaret.

We were all ready to go on, naked, when Freddie Mercury's manager appeared and said, 'You can't do the act.'

'What do you mean?' we asked. 'Why not?'

'We don't want you to go on,' he said.

'Why not?'

'We don't want Freddie Mercury to be associated with anything that might be considered gay,' he said.

'But we're not a gay act,' I said. 'And, anyway, he *is* gay. He's got a pink suit on. The band's called Queen.'

The manager looked at me.

'It doesn't matter,' I said. 'I don't care. But he *is* gay and everyone knows. It doesn't matter.'

They wouldn't let us do the Balloon Dance, but they paid us anyway and we pocketed £600. I said to the manager, 'Can we at least go to the party?'

'No,' he said. 'Not until Freddie's cut the cake.'

A few minutes later, a big pink cake was wheeled into the club. It was about twelve feet long and shaped like a Rolls-Royce with an FM-1 number-plate. They brought it in and laid it across three tables. Freddie Mercury posed with a knife for the photographers and stabbed at it. Then he buggered off into some other room. I said, 'Can we go to the party *now*?'

Yes, we were told, we could go to the party – but we couldn't go to the bit where all the Stars were. I started to feel bitter. I had wanted to do the Balloon Dance. I couldn't. I had wanted to meet all the stars. I couldn't. We ended up in this big room, where there were a load of hangers-on just hanging on and a pint of beer cost about three quid. I said to the other two, 'Let's fuck off.'

As we walked along the corridor towards the door, we saw Freddie Mercury's birthday cake. 'We'll have that!' I said. So we lifted it – heavy! – up a few stairs and put it in the back of our van. We pushed it in as far as we could but about four feet of it stuck out of the back. I had to drive from Xenon in the West End all the way home to South East London with that cake sticking out of the back of the van. I lived in a top-floor flat and, when we got to my place, we couldn't even get it through the front door of the house. We decided to take it round to Martin's: he lived on the ground floor. But the cake wouldn't fit through *his* door either and we had to take out his window.

At nine the next morning Louis Parker rang up. 'You bastards! You've stolen Freddie Mercury's birthday cake! It's worth four thousand and they've told the police.'

'Oh dear!' I said. I was genuinely worried, especially with my record, but Martin's bright and he's a good lateral thinker. It was coming up to Christmas so he said, 'We'll give it to a local old people's home. Old folks like cake.'

We phoned up the Ranyard Memorial Nursing Home and offered them a big cake and they said they'd have it. Then, same thing in reverse. Window out. Cake in the back of the Luton Transit. We drove off, gave the cake to the old people and I went back to my house and had some well-deserved sleep.

At about four that afternoon, two CID officers came to my door and said, 'You've nicked Freddie Mercury's birthday cake.'

'I haven't,' I said. 'Honestly.'

So then – and this is God's honest truth – they came into my house and crawled around the floor with magnifying glasses searching for crumbs. To this day, I haven't been caught.

Also as a result of the Balloon Dance and *OTT*, we toured Sweden, which was another experience altogether. Swedish culture seemed dull. We played big places called dance restaurants. Everyone went to them – grandparents, middle-aged couples, teenage children – and they were like big wedding receptions with bands like good wedding bands who played every type of music. A punk number would be followed by a waltz followed by rock 'n' roll. Each dance restaurant had a decibel monitoring machine like a set of traffic lights. If a musician wanted to play something loudly, the green light would go orange and then, if he kept playing loudly, it would go red and then all the music cut out.

Each Swedish town offered a choice of two department stores and, in each, all the clothes were exactly the same. The Swedes are *very* dull and, to this day, I don't know why they liked us.

There was a TV programme – like their version of *Saturday Night Live* – called *Noyamachine: The Entertainment Machine*. The producers had seen our Balloon Dance on *OTT* and wanted to show a clip on their programme. Central Television, however, insisted they buy the whole edition of *OTT* so the Swedes paid about £40,000 just to show the Balloon Dance. To get their money's worth, they showed it on *Noyamachine* every week as a sort of running gag. As a consequence, we were famous all over Sweden. They had 'Ballongen Dance' competitions and they released a pop record, with three lookalikes of us on the front cover, which reached number one in the Swedish hit parade. I knew none of this before we arrived.

When I'd accepted the booking in Sweden, I thought it was going to be like our tour of Holland – with hills and snow – but it became plain that something was up as soon as we got off the plane in Stockholm. There was a red carpet, television cameras were in evidence and we were taken to the airport VIP lounge. That night, we saw the news on Swedish TV: 'Arriving in Sweden today was President Brezhnev of Russia and also the Ballongen Dancers.' And there we were on the telly, coming off the plane.

The only problem with Swedish women is their names. In one week, I ended up with a Doris, an Agnes and a Maude. They were all young and beautiful, but it still seemed like shagging your grandmother.

The Swedes loved the Greatest Show on Legs and we seemed to appeal to all ages. The downside was that we had to judge a couple on their Ballongen Dance competitions. They had big fat blokes getting drunk, smiling a lot and doing it like a rugby club mooning exercise rather than the subtle and sophisticated thing we British know and love. The Swedes didn't understand the humour. Today Mr Methane, a British 'farteur', is very popular in their country.

We did *OTT* in January 1981 and our first Edinburgh Fringe in August 1982. That year, we played in a venue called the Hole in the Ground: an 'organisation' called Circuit had erected a huge marquee on a piece of derelict wasteland. Also performing there was the Egg Man, an Icelander, whose act consisted of a two-hour monologue in Icelandic, to an audience of one in the cave that gave the Hole in the Ground its name. He auctioned the ticket for each show and a reviewer from the *Scotsman* had to pay over fifty pounds to watch a performance. He couldn't understand a word but it was Art.

Several other shows were running at the Hole in the Ground, including the National Revue Company, with Arthur Smith, Phil Nice, Adam Wide and 'Joy Pickles' played by Babs Sutton, who lived with Martin Soan for two or three years. Much later she was hit and concussed by a beer glass thrown at my London club the

Tunnel. I became good friends with Arthur Smith, whose real name is Brian. That first year in Edinburgh, we were both doing sketch-related stuff. In a way, our paths have been similar. We are roughly the same age. Arthur lives in Balham now, but he grew up near me and went to school in Greenwich. He went to the University of East Anglia to study drama and I went to prison. Not much difference there.

After the National Revue Company broke up, Arthur formed Fiasco Job Job with Phil Nice and then went on to become the living legend that he is today. We both ended up as compères. I'm more coarse than he is, but he's more talented, particularly because of his playwriting. Years ago he asked me to put a thousand pounds into *An Evening With Gary Lineker*. I said yes because, at the time, I was almost flush with money, but he never came back to me. It was a big success all round the world. One minute you're drinking the wine, the next you're treading the grapes.

Arthur and I have been on the same bill many times, though we have never performed together as an act. We're too similar: he needs an Ernie Wise-type straight man and I need a Martin Soan – who is not a straight man as such, but he is surreal and the complete opposite to my stage character, the earthy comic.

That first year, the Circuit tent in Edinburgh held about 700 people. I had stupidly agreed we'd do our show for a 'wage' of £500 a week. In the meantime, we'd been on *OTT*, we were popular and they were selling tickets at a fiver each. The company was making around £3,500 a night and we were getting £500 a week between the three of us. I felt bitter again.

A group of feminists called Monstrous Regiment was also on at the Hole in the Ground. They were doing a play about prisoners, about how it's not the cons' fault they're in jail, it's society's fault, or it's all of our faults. All that nonsense.

That first year we were really poor. We were performing in the Tent in the Hole in the Ground and we were living in tents next to the Tent. Edinburgh is always cold and it was even colder that year. It snowed.

Also that year a German opera show had a pig in it and my tent was next to where they kept the pig.

At the end of the week, Circuit held a press conference and put up *another* tent. A big marquee. Commissionaire outside. Posh. We turned up and they wouldn't let us in, even though we'd been there a week and sold out our shows. Well, we *were* naked, which might have had something to do with it. And not entirely wholesome. When we got dressed they eventually agreed to let us in. But I was still bitter.

It was a bit of a posh do, with wine and little bits of food. Monstrous Regiment were there but their feminist dungarees were off and their public-school cocktail dresses were on. One of them got her handbag nicked. She went berserk. 'Catch him!' she yelled. 'Get the police! I want that man put in prison!'

I said to her, 'It's not his fault. It's society's fault. It's all our faults.'

When the press conference proper started, they asked one person from each show to get up on the bar and give a speech to the assembled journalists. The Monstrous Regiment woman had calmed down. She stood on the bar and said, 'We're doing a play about prisoners. It's a scathing indictment of society.'

Then it was the German with the pig. He said, 'We're doing an opera with a pig.'

We were next and I got on the bar, having briefed Martin. 'Well, ladies and gentlemen of the press,' I began, 'we're the Greatest Show on Legs and we have a bit of a comedy show in that tent over there, but this is no night for comedy because I've just read in the paper that the great Glenda Jackson has passed away and, in the spirit of the Fringe' – a real tear trickled out of my eye – 'I'd like to ask for one minute's silence for a great actress.'

Silence.

I looked at my watch and the whole minute went by.

A long time.

Then Martin tugged at my trousers and handed up my newspaper to me. I looked at it.

'Oh!' I said. 'Not *Glenda* Jackson. *Wendy* Jackson. A pensioner from Sydenham . . . Doesn't matter then, does it?'

The tent fell even more silent than it had been during the minute's silence.

Finally a thespian at the front looked up at me and theatrically projected: 'Bad taste!' He was wearing a pink and green shirt.

This was the beginning of a beautiful, long-running relationship between the Edinburgh Fringe and me.

We went back next year, back to the Hole in the Ground. This time Circuit had *three* tents. They *loved* a tent. They had a big one in the middle, with a small one on one side and a medium one on the other. Like Daddy Tent, Mummy Tent and Baby Tent. You could pay to see one show and hear all three as they ran simultaneously.

We were in the Daddy Tent, Emma Thompson was in the little one with the Emma Thompson Band and in the other was an American called Eric Bogosian. Later he starred in Oliver Stone's movie *Talk Radio*. I never got on with him. He was a prima donna. He upset everyone. He upset Emma Thompson. She was in tears and, boldly, I told him to leave her alone. But all the arguments and artistic friction stemmed from the clash of noise.

We tried to arrange it so that we all did our noisy bits at the same time. Then, with luck, the audiences wouldn't be distracted. But Eric was having none of it. One part of his show had heavy metal music in our quiet bit. His show was called *Funhouse – An Anarchistic Romp through the American Way of Life*. So, I thought, if he's a bit of an anarchist he'll like a laugh, won't he?

Our show opened with me entering on a tractor. I tried to leap over ten toy cars but, of course, the tractor went off the ramp and squashed the cars. Good opening. We had persuaded the manager of a local garden centre to lend us the tractor in exchange for us advertising his business. He was in the audience with his family the night I decided to visit Eric Bogosian. We had had about six days of Eric's heavy metal coming through into our show and that night, when Eric started up the usual hell of a row with his tape, I screamed at our audience – to make myself heard above the noise, 'Look, we'll go and see Eric. All of us. He'll like it. He's a bit of a laugh. He's an anarchist.'

I jumped on the tractor, naked, drove out of our tent straight into his and on to his stage. Our audience followed behind. 'Hello, Eric!' I said.

He was swaying backwards and forwards, air-guitaring with a broom handle in his hands going 'Brrrrrmmmmmmm!' to an AC/DC track that was coming out of the loudspeakers. Very witty, I presume.

When he saw me – in the nude on the tractor followed by all our audience – he flopped into a chair at the back of the stage. We all filed past him, came out of his tent, went back into our own and thought no more about it.

After about two minutes, I heard the sound of a tractor being smashed up with a sledgehammer. Then I heard, round the back, all the dressing rooms being wrecked. Then he came running in. By this time, Martin Soan was naked and I had clothes on. Eric saw Martin and thought he was me so he hit him, knocked him over and ran out screaming. Martin got up and carried on, because we've had worse than that.

The next day, all hell broke loose with Circuit. Eric claimed it was all my fault. Well, I suppose it *was*, really. They fined us eight hundred pounds because we had to refund all the people who had walked out of Eric's show. I found out later that this included all the people who'd walked out of his show before my intervention.

I was bitter again. We were still living in tents and he had this house with thick carpets where I was made to go and apologise. I did – *a bit*.

Two years after the tractor episode, I was sitting at home in Greenwich watching Channel 4 when the announcer said: 'Appearing live at nine at the Albany Empire on *Loose Talk*, Eric Bogosian.' The Albany Empire was about two miles from where I was sitting, so I thought, I'll go and see Eric again!

A mate of mine, Mad Mick, works for a fork-lift truck company. I phoned him up and said, 'Can I borrow a fork-lift truck? I've got a friend on at the Albany Empire and I want to pay him a visit.'

'All right,' he said.

I got the fork-lift and drove to the Albany. It takes about twenty minutes in a fork-lift truck. I poised myself outside at nine o'clock, ready to go in. I took off my clothes. Then, dead on nine – whoosh – straight into the Albany with the fork-lift truck.

But I'd got the night wrong and it was an aerobics class for the over-fifties.

The Fringe gets to you after a while. It makes you do funny things. The funniest thing I ever heard in Edinburgh involved a coach driver. It was the end of the eighties and I was a bit depressed, because it was the third or fourth week of the Fringe – everyone gets the Fringe blues around then: you've done two or three weeks of constant shows and drinking and going to the Gilded Balloon after your own show and partying – so I went out, one cold Edinburgh day, and that *is* cold, and saw one of those open-topped tourist buses.

Downstairs it was full of pensioners who smelt of urine, so I sat upstairs. It was a pleasant tour and the driver had a microphone giving all the old tourist nonsense: 'On the right there's the

Castle and on the left is where wee Rabbie Burns . . .' and so on until, half-way along Princes Street, a car cut him up and he forgot about the microphone. 'On the right there's the Castle and – fuck off ya fuckin' bastard! Ya fuckin' cunt!' Pity I wasn't downstairs – but I could imagine the faces of all those pensioners.

Arthur Smith does his own guided tour of Edinburgh every year on the last night of the Fringe and I'm always on it. It lasts from four o'clock on the Sunday morning to seven o'clock or arrest by the police, whichever comes first. I'm always paralytic by the end but I have to get the nine a.m. train to London as on the Sunday night, I always perform in my London club.

After one of Arthur Smith's tours, I found myself in a hotel with a well-known journalist, who used to be the fashion editor of *Vogue* – she was in her early fifties and I must have been thirty-eight. Wizo woke me up at eight the next morning to get the train. I was shagged out and, luckily, got a carriage to myself. I sat down and thought, This is it! I'm going to go to sleep. But, just as I dropped off, a couple of hundred Scottish football supporters got on, all with cans of lager, shouting, 'Ya bastards! Ya English bastards!' and the traditional crying baby arrived.

On his tour, Arthur offers various sums of money to various people along the route to do various things. Somehow I've always managed to get twenty-five pounds for standing up naked and singing 'Scotland the Brave'. The police are usually summoned, but what Arthur hasn't known – and won't until he reads this – is that three times I've called the police myself. I've used the phone box half-way down the Royal Mile to tell them there's a madman on the loose. Once I was arrested in the name of Arthur Smith outside the Gilded Balloon. He was in the same group as me but I was peeing against a wall when the police stopped me. 'Right! We're arresting you for urinating in a public place. Name and address!'

I gave Arthur's and I've never heard from them since. I don't know if he has.

Most people pay to get into shows at the Edinburgh Fringe. I don't encourage this. The thing to do is to buy a little plastic sheath from a stationer's, get a bit of card and some Letraset, write PRESS in big letters, then REVIEWER in smaller letters, and your name at the bottom. You put the card inside the plastic sheath, iron it (a domestic iron does the job just fine) and you've got a press card. It'll take you anywhere.

I did this for the Snakebite Award. The Perrier Award has been presented at the Edinburgh Fringe for about ten years to the best comedy/cabaret performance. It is organised by a woman with the unfortunate name of Nica Burns. Unfortunate, because 'Nica' is pronounced 'Knicker'.

My Snakebite Award was the opposite of the Perrier Award, and presented for the worst cabaret. I made a few cards, gave them to pals and we saw any show we fancied for free. I went to a Japanese opera at the Playhouse Theatre. I didn't understand a word but I hadn't paid to see it.

The Snakebite Award's first prize was worth a thousand pounds, so it almost always had to be given to someone I knew well, or someone who wouldn't ask for the money. I won it a couple of times and Chris Luby, from *The Mad Show*, has also carried off this supreme accolade. The London Hospital Medical School were outright winners the first two years running, once with an effort called *Jean de Toilette*, the worst show I have *ever* seen. They performed a musical number called 'Flush Gordon', a rip-off of Queen's similarly entitled song, at the point in the plot where the hero, Jean, is sitting on a toilet cleaning his teeth with a lavatory brush, surrounded by a bevy of nurses in stockings and suspenders. I watched it with a bloke called Tristram Davies from the *Independent*, who said it was the funniest thing he'd ever seen. We couldn't stop laughing, but we were laughing *at* rather than *with*. We almost had to be carried out. The venue was the lecture theatre of a psychiatric hospital in Morningside, on the outskirts of Edinburgh, and it was packed. It was a Monday and three hundred people turned up. My show was right in the middle of town and I was performing to about thirty people each night. Proves something, though exactly what I don't know.

For their first win, I gave the Medical School a cheque for five hundred pounds. It bounced but they were happy with that. Then I felt guilty, because they *are* a hospital, so I did a gig at the London Hospital, charged five hundred pounds and gave the fee to the medical school.

A lot of people thought and think alternative comedy, like some poetry, preaches to people or is doing some worthwhile job in a vaguely left wing way.

But I remember playing a small place called the Comedy Boom at the Edinburgh Fringe in the mid-eighties. I was compèring a show featuring musical comedy group Skint Video, comic/poet John Hegley and Sensible Footwear, a three-woman feminist group. The landlady's daughter was about twenty-three and watched every show because she was there clearing glasses up. She laughed very loudly and genuinely at each show. I used to do a joke competition where members of the audience submitted their own jokes and, after about a week of this, she came up to me and said: 'I've got a joke for you.'

The joke was something about 'a nigger with a parrot on his shoulder'.

She thought I could actually get up on stage and tell that joke after watching a week's worth of right-on alternative comedy.

I suppose the Greatest Show on Legs did veer slightly towards the left on stage. There's no politics in the act but we veered towards the left because we didn't do what right wing comedians did. We did not come on in frilly shirts and bow ties. We've always come on in jeans, looking unshaven. And we did lots of Benefits for left wing causes like Save the Whales. In fact, I think we *have* saved the whale: I saw one the other day on telly.

125

CHAPTER 8

JO, FRANK, JOOLS AND BLOWJOBS

T he Glastonbury Festival was the brainchild of Michael Eaves, the man who owns the land on which it is held. He's accused of making lots of money out of it now but I don't know that he does. He's a Quaker and says he doesn't need it: he gets a good enough income off his cows. (Maybe he'll think differently now that BSE has made its mark.) I reckon he does it because he likes the spirit of it. But it *has* changed – the first time I went to Glastonbury, there was just one tent with music and comedy and everything. Now there's acres of it.

We first went down there in 1978 with the Box Brothers, who toured Holland with us. Their guitarist Mark Flanagan now plays with the Jools Holland Band, while Ronnie Box is sound mixer. Paul Fitzgerald has his own recording studio in Norfolk and works a lot for the BBC.

Pip had found out about my affair with Mandy Moy because Ronnie Box, who fancied Pip, told her. Before we moved back to London, he'd been to Canterbury to pledge his troth and casually dropped into the conversation something like, 'So you don't mind Malcolm sleeping with all these girls?'

Pip confronted me with this at the Man in the Moon and I owned up to Mandy but not to the two girls I knew in Holland.

Pip threw a cup of coffee over me – no sugar.

The Box Brothers also had a drummer called Bootsie, whose enthusiasm for personal chemistry was extensive, and an attractive girl singer, Delphi Newman, whose dad was a record producer. After the Box Brothers split up, she fancied getting off with the singer Ian Dury but she didn't know where he lived. About five years ago, I gave her a lift from Norfolk to London, and two weeks later she was living with him.

The Glastonbury Festival's cabaret and children's events are organised by Arabella Churchill, who looks like her grandfather Winston and is very laid back. She married a juggler called Haggis.

Before her marriage I got off with her because she had a big warm house and I was fed up living in a field.

I remember putting on an American comedian at Glastonbury. He was called Barry Diamond, a sharp Los Angeles/Las Vegas comedy-circuit mohair-suit act. He was a very good pre-Gerry Sadowitz act – politically incorrect but funny. His manager was Miles Copeland, who also managed rock bands Police and Squeeze and was the son of the man who helped found the CIA. Miles Copeland and Barry Diamond turned up in a limousine at the entrance to the Glastonbury Festival which, at that time, was just a hippie at a gate with a straw bale. They didn't have a pass and the hippie said, 'Oh, wow! Hey, man, I'll have to go and check.'

They ignored him, revved the engine, drove through the straw bale and came to the comedy tent. Miles Copeland and Barry Diamond. Two American showbiz types. Completely out of place.

Arabella was lying on three bean-bags. Miles asked her what time Barry was on and she said, 'We-e-ll. We-e-e-e-e-ll . . . Might be four. Might be five. Might be ten. I'm not sure, man. Peace.'

Miles picked her up by the collar of her dress and said, 'What time's he on, ya bitch?'

This made Arabella sharpen up a bit and Barry performed at four in the afternoon to an unsuitable audience of six-year-olds.

The Greatest Show on Legs have always been successful at Glastonbury – and more about that later.

When Martin Clarke, who had appeared on *OTT* with us, moved to Hong Kong we recruited Jonty Wright from Norfolk and Steve Bowditch from South East London. I found Steve when I was walking along the road by my house and saw him inside a recording studio, where he was making tea. I liked the look of his face so I went in and said to him, 'Do you want to be in a show?'

'Yes,' he said.

He came round that afternoon, rehearsed about three

numbers and next day he was in Rhyl, North Wales, performing with the Greatest Show on Legs.

In 1983, the four of us went up to Edinburgh and linked up with Skint Video, a group of musical political parodists – a bit like the Barron Knights with teeth. One of them did the Balloon Dance with us and we took on a couple of their sketches. We toured together for about a year.

I didn't care much about political correctness and left-wing causes, but some people did. Once we were booked at a university but, when we got there, it turned out there were strippers on the bill, too. Skint Video refused to go on. In the end, the Greatest Show on Legs took a vote on it and we didn't go on either because working with strippers was meant to be demeaning to women. Ironic that we had been set to do the Balloon Dance in which one member of Skint Video had been going to perform naked. But girl strippers were different apparently.

Another time, we were offered a South African mini-tour in the days of apartheid. I said we should take it because we had to see for ourselves what it was like. But I was outvoted on that one too.

I have always felt like an outsider. Even at the Edinburgh Fringe. There, I was the wrong side of the Fringe. And we were always broke too. Once, when I was really poor in Edinburgh, I saw a wage packet lying on the ground in the Circuit site. It contained two hundred pounds. I went *whoosh* – into my pocket. Conscience pricked. I thought, It's someone's wages. There was a name on the packet, but we didn't know him. I should have handed it in. But we didn't have any money. I vacillated. I asked Martin what I should do and he came up with a good idea: go down to the bookmaker's, put the money on a horse and, if the horse won, we'd give the wages back. If the horse lost, we'd all have lost. So I did. This was before bookies had telly screens. They had a loudspeaker system with a voice that, of course, had a Scottish accent. I misunderstood the accent and backed the wrong horse, put the money on an animal that I *thought* was 7–2. But it was actually 17–2. For 7–2 you got nine hundred pounds; at 17–2 you got nineteen hundred.

By some miracle, it won.

No, I didn't give the money back.

At around this point Wizo, who had been off the scene for about five years – marriage, a demanding career working in an exhaust and car spares shop – turned up again as our roadie. He had settled down to a standard suburban life in Bromley and, whenever I went to see him, there was always an element of 'Oh! Here's Malcolm! I'm going to be in trouble!'

He was only meant to be our roadie.

We had a spotlight on a stick and all he had to do was set up the microphone. Then there was a bit in the show where he had to move the microphone – we couldn't do it because we were getting changed for the next sketch. After about four or five shows, however, he didn't just move the microphone, he started speaking into it, saying, 'Hello. My name's Wizo,' and trying to tell jokes. Eventually, he was performing in our sketches and appeared on TV programmes like *The Tube*. People get into showbiz in the strangest ways.

Before she became a comedienne, Jo Brand and her friend Sue used to be big fans of Skint Video and used to go to lots of their shows. They used to follow Skint Video and us about. They were a bit comedy-groupie-ish. Jo and I had an 'affair' for a couple of years, when I was living with Pip.

Jo was a psychiatric nurse. At that time, my sister Clare went 'radio rental' – she'd gone barmy once before but hadn't been hospitalised. She has a hypermania that is triggered off about every four years. The second time it happened, she was found walking round Victoria station saying she *was* Queen Victoria. We took her to the doctor, then to casualty and, when we were signing

131

her into the Maudsley Psychiatric Hospital, Jo Brand was the nurse admitting her. I heard later that, when I came in with Clare, the other nurses were more worried about the look of me.

The last time Clare went mad, in 1994 – it's the World Cup starts her off, I think – she ended up in Hither Green Psychiatric Hospital where there were patients in different degrees of madness. I was chatting to one who seemed reasonably normal and said to him, 'This is my sister.'

'Is it really?' he said. 'That *is* strange, a brother and sister both being in here at the same time.'

While I was going out with her, Jo bought a piano, which I took as a sign of her being stagestruck. After I heard her play the Moonlight Sonata, I said, "You should do comedy on stage." I don't say that lightly to people because hosts of people are the Funniest Person in the Pub but can't transfer it to the stage. I don't know exactly why I thought Jo could: maybe because she had a certain confidence and there was that deadpan delivery. She was very monotone when she first started. Still is, slightly. But I didn't help her deliver her lines better. She did it herself. She became very good very quickly. I didn't get involved with her professionally because I didn't want her to feel I was latching on to her success. I didn't see her first spot, at the Meccano club in North London, but her second or third was in Greenwich, which she did very well. She always went down a storm with a rough audience. She once had the heckle, just thirty seconds into her act, '*Don't* show us yer tits!'

She kept her job as a psychiatric nurse for at least a couple of years at the start of her career in comedy, then decided to chuck in the job and become a comic when she found she was making as much – or more – on stage. I advised her to give up her job.

I've advised a few people to do that. I told Frank Skinner he wasn't going to get anywhere unless he gave up his job as an assistant drama lecturer. When he was going to be on *This Is Your*

Life, I got a message on my answerphone on the Friday afternoon from a researcher saying they wanted me to be at the London Palladium at eleven o'clock on the Sunday night. That Friday I had a bit to drink, as you do. I brought a few people back to my house, including someone called Tom from the West Country. I told them all I was going to Frank Skinner's *This Is Your Life* and the comedian Jim Tavare said: 'Why don't you just ring him up and tell him?' It seemed time to give Frank another bit of good advice.

I didn't have Frank's home phone number but I phoned up Rob Newman at about four o'clock in the morning. Rob thought it sounded like a good idea because, at the time, he wasn't getting on very well with David Baddiel, his former double-act partner who now shares a flat with Frank Skinner.

I rang up Frank's answerphone and said in a West Country voice, " 'Ello there, Frank Skinner. When that Michael Aspel comes up to you with that big red book, tell him to *fuck off*!" As far as I know, he heard it, but they convinced him it was a hoax.

When I got to the Palladium, I was going to go on and say, 'Frank Skinner? Oh, yeah, he's brilliant since he got rid of that beret and stopped doing that *Oooh, Betty!* stuff.' But they didn't have me on: I just sat in the audience. So I had one of my bitter turns again and, at the party after the show, I was a bit drunk. I introduced myself to Michael Aspel and started talking about pressure points. Then I squeezed the back of his neck and he didn't go *right* down on the floor but he buckled a bit. He didn't say anything but he looked shocked. Then I wandered over to Jenny Eclair and got ushered out by two big Palladium gorillas in blue coats.

I tried to get a taxi home from Regent Street and hailed two black cabs but I was so drunk I couldn't say 'Greenwich'. They both drove away. So I hailed a third cab and said, 'New Cross.'

*

Back in 1983 the Greatest Show on Legs got fed up with touring and split up as a full-time act. But we're a bit like the folk group Fairport Convention: we keep having reunions. When we stopped being the Greatest Show on Legs full-time, I started the Tunnel Palladium, an early alternative-comedy venue.

Every year we did two Greatest Show on Legs pub crawls. We selected four or five South East London pubs where we'd go and give a show for free. We did one pub crawl in the winter, round Christmas, and one in the summer. One pub we went to was the Mitre in a rough area of Greenwich, about fifty yards from the southern exit of the Blackwall Tunnel. Our show there was on a Sunday night and we couldn't give it for free because the landlord insisted it was a condition of his licence that he had to charge an entrance fee. I think he charged two pounds a head.

The show at the Mitre was packed. The pub had been divided into two bars. We performed in one and in the other a stag night was going on in honour of the local constabulary. But it wasn't just a stag night. They had strippers who performed full sex. They were giving blowjobs and wiping the result on the beer mats. I went into this bar and was sitting next to a copper who thought I was part of the stag-night crowd. In front of me was a stripper sucking a bloke's knob. I said to the copper, 'What's that all about?'

'Oh,' he said, 'that's all right. He's getting married tomorrow.'

After that night, I spoke to the woman. She said she recognised me because she used to go out with my mate Dexie Doug Davies. It all came back to me in a flash: I remembered Dexie Doug complaining that this woman, Frances was her name, wouldn't go the whole way but spent 90 per cent of her waking hours giving him blowjobs. (I've heard complaints about other relationships, but they were the exact opposite.)

It was an odd experience. Two different audiences: a lot of trendy lefties watching the Greatest Show on Legs in one bar, and, in the other, a load of coppers being serviced by strippers.

The next Sunday I went back. There was a heavy metal band on with about four people in the audience – friends of the band. I said, 'Last week, when we were here, there were three hundred people. What's going on?' And I ended up, at the suggestion of Steve Black who was the pub's rock promoter, running a Sunday comedy club at the Mitre.

I named it the Tunnel because it was next to the Blackwall Tunnel. Strangely enough, the landlord had tunnel vision. But that was just an odd coincidence.

Martin Potter, who had helped up on the pilot for *OTT* and the audition for *Game for a Laugh*, became my partner for our Sunday Night at the Tunnel Palladium shows. We made some promotional flyers and the club was an instant success. Our first show, on 8 January 1984, featured the cream of alternative comedy talent. We had Steve Bowditch compèring as a character called Wilbert, a verbal precursor to Mr Bean. The acts included Ronnie Golden, Fiasco Job Job (Arthur Smith and Phil Nice) and Skint Video, the comedy trio who, after that night, became a comedy duo. They had a row on stage.

The next week, Steve couldn't do the compèring but as he didn't tell me until the day of the show I had to do it, and continued every Sunday from 1984 to 1989. I even flew back from Edinburgh at Festival time to do Sunday Night at the Tunnel Palladium.

It was a starting-point for lots of people, like Harry Enfield and Jo Brand. We even contributed thirty pounds to Paul Merton's now millionaire bank account. Alexei Sayle, Rik Mayall and Ade Edmondson felt they were too big to play the Tunnel but Nigel Planer appeared in the month he had a No. 1 hit with 'Hole In My Shoe'. That night, people were trying to get in through the windows. When I started running the Tunnel, I became a local personality, which I enjoyed.

I had been inside for most of the seventies so I had missed

all the music scene, but my sister had been out with the bass player from Squeeze and I met Jools Holland at a party. Jools knew that Martin and I did a Punch and Judy show, but he hadn't seen it. Soon after we met him, he said, 'I could do with a Punch and Judy show for my son's fourth birthday party.'

That was a big mistake. We did have a *sort-of* children's version. It had Punch pissing, whereas the adult version showed him having a wank.

At the beginning of the children's version, I would say, 'We want to see Mr Punch!'

To which Martin would respond, 'I'm not coming out!'

'Why not?' I'd ask.

'Because I want to have a piss,' he'd say.

'What did you say?' I'd ask.

'I want to 'ave a fuckin' piss!' he'd say.

Then Martin, inside the booth with a bottle of yellow Squeezy washing-up liquid, would squirt it out all over the audience. The kids normally liked that.

What happened at Jools's son's party was that I scared the life out of these poor kids. Martin couldn't be there, so I borrowed the puppets from him and had to do the puppeteering, the speaking, the whole lot. And I couldn't do it properly because I'm not very dextrous. When I squeezed the Squeezy bottle, instead of the usual thin jet arcing across the room, the top came off and the whole lot spurted out. The living room was soaked and some went into the grand piano.

When Mr Punch appeared on the playboard, the younger kids all ran out of the room. Mr Punch is quite scary when you're three or four. His head was nearly human size, made of foam. And it was noisy: the clattering of cymbals coupled with the Acme Thunderer whistle. The show was rather short. About five minutes all told. But Jools didn't mind. He still came to the Mitre to see Sunday Night at the Tunnel Palladium.

John Rowlan, the landlord of the Mitre, wasn't a brilliant businessman. I originally paid him about fifty pounds to rent the room. Then, when he saw it was successful, *he* started giving *me* fifty pounds and, without me even asking, he gave me 10 per cent of the bar takings.

John was about forty. He lived above the pub with his wife Val, a daughter who got married to some right herbert, and a son, Simon. They were like an inbred gypsy family and some Hell's Angels motor mechanics set up a garage round the back. Simon was in charge of promoting the music. He wasn't great on business either – once he had hundreds of posters printed with a band's name and the Tunnel. No address. No date. No time. His other triumph was Siouxsie and the Banshees. The band was very successful then and their tour manager came in and said Siouxsie wanted to do an anonymous 'secret' gig at the Tunnel just before she went off on a big European tour. So the son didn't tell *anyone*. The band turned up to an audience of half a dozen and her crew.

In the fifties and sixties, the Mitre had been a well-known jazz pub. John had found a lot of photographs down in the cellar of Bing Crosby, Duke Ellington and Spike Milligan among others, all signed by the stars and saying things like: 'Thank you to the Mitre pub.'

I saw him a week later and he'd thrown them away. He said, 'I didn't want all those old photos.' He'd probably been sitting on a goldmine. It wasn't that he was eccentric. He just didn't have a clue about anything – and especially not about alternative comedy. He suggested putting on people like Jimmy Jones and Jim Davidson.

The pub was tied to Courage but whether he bought Courage beer or not I don't know because often when we went back to clear up on a Monday morning Whitbread lorries were delivering barrels. Under the Rowlan family's careful administration, the Mitre was probably the worst pub in the world.

During the early days of alternative comedy, however, several acts passed through the Tunnel who needed an agent to get work for them. I knew the venues because I'd performed at them with the Greatest Show on Legs so I became an agent for dozens of acts, including people like Jeremy Hardy and Harry Enfield when they were just starting.

The first thing I had to do was make a brochure to send to venues. Jools Holland agreed to go into it because by now he was a mate of mine. I did a couple of tours for him and put him on at Edinburgh successfully four times on the trot. Then he had a bad accident doing a charity gig in Plymouth that I hadn't been involved in setting up for him. He and his band were driving back from the gig when it happened. In the front of the car were John Lay, the tour manager, and Gilson Lavis, the excellent drummer who had been with Squeeze before Jools. In the back, furtively, because he was then living with someone else, were Jools and Lady Christabel Durham, his current partner. They had a head-on collision at about 70 m.p.h. on the M4. Lady Christabel broke her leg, the drummer and the tour manager were badly injured but Jools was unscathed. They all ended up in Exeter hospital.

By coincidence, that day I was going to see the social secretary of Exeter University about putting Jools on as part of the forth-coming tour I was arranging. As I arrived in Exeter station, I noticed Jools in a train going back the way I'd come. I found out what had happened and went to the hospital. When I saw John Lay, he could hardly speak but muttered mysteriously, 'Don't say anything about Lady Christabel.'

This was all Greek to me as I was then unaware of Jools's liaison with her, as was his live-in lover, who was on her way to Exeter, not knowing that Jools had left the hospital. She didn't discover Lady Christabel there, but eventually it all came out in the wash.

When I got back to London, I said to Jools, 'Well, that's it!

We can't do the tour now because we haven't got a drummer or a tour manager.'

'Do you know any drummers?' he asked.

I mentioned a man called Rowland Rivron, who played the drums with a parody band called Raw Sex. Jools auditioned him and they hit it off straightaway.

Then Jools said, 'Do you know anyone who can do the tour-managing?'

'I'll do it,' I said.

Then he said, 'We'll need a support act.'

'I'll do it,' I said.

I ended up being the tour manager, the support act as a stand-up comic, the agent *and* played the harmonica with the band in the last two numbers every night. I earned more than Jools!

Being tour manager for Jools Holland was completely different from tour-managing the Greatest Show on Legs. He wanted hotels, time schedules, sound checks, the works. All a comedian needs are a microphone, his clothes and a modicum of talent.

On that tour in the summer of 1986, we did a gig in Dartmoor prison, which was a bit unsettling. Although I'm no stranger to the Wonderful World of Jail, I always feel a touch nervous when I see all those bars and gates and dogs. It was an odd gig altogether because the whole thing was run by the chaplain. He was exactly like the vicar in *Dad's Army* – almost his double. They'd screened off the back area from the stage so we couldn't see any of the cons. We just heard a rattling of keys and them all filing in. Jools said to the chaplain, 'What are the prisoners like as an audience?'

The chaplain, who was also going to be the compère, replied, 'Well, I expect when I go onstage there will be a little bit of tittle-tattle, but don't you worry about that. Then you'll be on.' He went out on stage and said, 'Gentlemen –'

And all hell broke loose.

'Fuck off! Fuck off, you wanker! Fuck off!' came from five hundred voices simultaneously.

A little bit of tittle-tattle. Right. He carried on, in a gentle, caring voice, 'Now, now, boys. Remember your parole,' then introduced the band. They loved Jools – but they definitely didn't like the chaplain.

Showbiz!

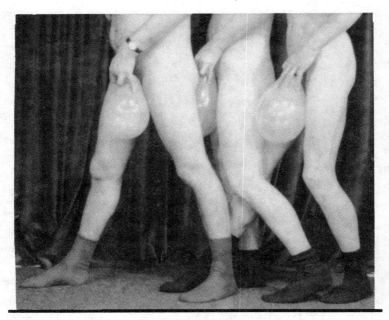

CHAPTER 9

BIRTH AND DEATH

My first child, Frank, was born in December 1985. He hadn't
been planned by me but Pip, who was fast approaching thirty,
wanted a baby. I remember the birth rather clearly. Pip was in the
audience at the Albany Empire in Deptford and I was compèring in
a leopardskin coat and a pair of white winkle-picker shoes. Bob
Jones, head of Greenwich Leisure Services, was there. Half-way
through my act, he tugged at my trousers and said, 'She's gone
into labour!'

He drove her to the hospital, then came back to the Albany
to pick me up. I went straight there without changing. It was
getting on for midnight. I'd been to all the antenatal classes, but
I hadn't realised how long it would take. I was sitting with Pip in
the delivery room for a good two hours without a cigarette. Eventually I had to go downstairs for a fag. When I came back there was
all this screaming going on. I went into the delivery room: five
people were crowded round the bed and I was trying to peer over
their shoulders. I still had my leopardskin coat on. In the end,
the baby was born and someone said, 'You've given birth to a
lovely baby girl. Well done, Heather!' I'd been in at the wrong
birth. I eased myself quickly out of the room and got back to Pip,
who gave birth to Frank after about another eleven hours.

I was there when he was born. I saw the whole body come
out and I thought he was dead because he was a bluish colour.
But then he started wriggling about and that was good. Moving. I
made loads of phone calls and got drunk.

That same week, my mother had a similar experience. She
had to go to an old friend's funeral and missed the cortège leaving
the house but saw it travelling towards Hither Green Crematorium.
She tagged on to the end and followed the mourners into the
chapel. She had been there for a good ten minutes before she
realised that the vicar was talking about a different person who
coincidentally had the same forename. Like me, she shuffled out

backwards and went into the next-door chapel just in time to see her friend's coffin disappear into the bowels of the furnace.

When Frank was about eight weeks old, Pip went back to work and I was left in charge of him at home. After I'd fed him I put him in his cot for a sleep. I was hungry so I popped out to Lil's Diner, a hundred yards down the street. I was sitting there eating when someone said, 'Malcolm! I hear you've had a baby boy!'

'Oh,' I said. 'So I have!' I got up slowly, went outside and then ran like hell back to the house. I'd forgotten about him.

When he was about three months old, Frank made his first stage appearance. I used him as a ventriloquist's dummy down at the Tunnel Palladium. He had perfect timing. I was announcing who was on and he was gurgling as I was saying their names. I got to the top act, a laconic Scottish comedian. I said, '. . . and Arnold Brown!' Frank yawned and fell asleep.

When Channel 4's rock show *The Tube* started, Jools Holland was one of the presenters. As we had become friends, he took me out for a meal to pick my brain about acts. I got Harry Enfield on the show. At the time, there was talk of him and me doing a double-act, which didn't come to anything. He was doing his pompous *Ooh, yes!* aristocratic character, which he'd got from a record I had of Gerard Hoffnung. We talked about performing as the Two Frankie Howerds. We were going to sit there and go, 'Oooaaargh, yeeees! No. Yes. Oooooh, Nooohh! Whhaaaatt?' for about ten minutes, then get off. I don't think it would have worked because I can't do characters. I can only be me. Some comedians can act; some can't. Tommy Cooper, who was a brilliant comedian, couldn't act. Whatever he did, whatever clothes he wore, he was always Tommy Cooper. People used to think that Tony Hancock was a brilliant actor but he *was* that character. Arthur Smith is always Arthur Smith. I'm always me.

Anyway, Jools took me out to Papillon restaurant in Greenwich and the meal cost £196 for four of us. At that time, I used to go to the Terminus Café opposite and get something for about £2.20 so I was impressed.

The Greatest Show on Legs were on *The Tube* six or seven times, though we never did the Balloon Dance. We did the Pop Musician's Lord's Prayer: 'Our Father who Art Garfunkel in Heaven 17 . . .', an Indiana Jones parody, several other favourites including the Human Fruit Machine and a Frank Sinatra sketch. It was Sinatra's birthday on one of the days *The Tube* was transmitted, so we wrapped Steve Bowditch from head to foot in bandages, put a Frank Sinatra hat on him and said, 'Unfortunately, the great man has had a bit of an accident but here he is – Frank Sinatra!'

Paula Yates, Jool's co-presenter, wouldn't speak to us after this because she said she was Sinatra's biggest fan. I sat next to her on the plane back from Newcastle, where *The Tube* was recorded, three times and tried to make conversation with her but she just stuck her nose in a copy of *Vogue* or whatever and wouldn't say a word. I got my own back a few years later when she interviewed me on Amnesty International's *Big 30* show, screened on ITV. She started asking questions and I looked up and said, 'Hello, Paula,' paused, then said, 'A serious case of mutton dressed as mutton.'

She scowled.

But generally I liked the attitude of the people on *The Tube*: producers Malcolm Gerrie and Geoff Wonfor were just Geordie lads, really.

After I'd appeared with the Greatest Show on Legs, they auditioned me for a job as presenter on *The Tube*. I nearly got it. It was down to me and a young kid called Felix. He was about fourteen, black, fashionable and sharp. He got it and he was fucking useless. No hard feelings, Felix. At the time, I fancied being presenter of *The Tube* because the opportunity came up just after Jools had been suspended for saying 'groovy fuckers' on a live trailer for the programme during children's television. Complaints flooded in. He denied it and claimed he'd said 'groovy fellahs', but unfortunately someone in the Midlands sent in a recording with a letter of complaint. Jools was suspended for four weeks.

I got various acts on to *The Tube*, but being an agent is a thankless task. An agent gets bookings for acts and takes 15 per cent of the fee. A manager normally acts as an agent but offers a lot more guidance on the artist's career and takes 20–30 per cent. Sometimes an artist has both agent and manager. A lot of agents are not appreciated by their clients because the clients, possibly quite rightly, think the agents don't do anything. Or, at least, nothing involving any talent or hard work. The client always thinks he's out there sweating away while the agent is making phone calls. Nothing could be further from the truth. There's all sorts of grief, and endless things go wrong, like people not turning up, wrong dates – it all happens.

When I was an agent, I went out and foraged for work for my acts because then there were only a few venues and comedy wasn't sought after. I produced five thousand brochures and sent them off to various places and rang up all the venues the Greatest Show on Legs had ever played. The first time I delved into management was with Gerry Sadowitz. I first saw him when he came down to the Tunnel Palladium. His act was brilliant. A breath of fresh air. He just launched into a tirade of abuse. This was at a time when, to be considered funny, all an alternative comedian had to do was to say that Mrs Thatcher was horrible and Barry Manilow had a big nose – which is, indeed, a Gerry Sadowitz line. Gerry came on stage at the Albany Empire in Deptford, which had an extremely politically correct arts centre audience. He started his act with, 'Nelson Mandela. What a cunt!'

He did it deliberately, of course, to upset that particular type of audience. And they *were* upset. He was on for two nights and, on the second, they picketed the place. It was all water off a duck's back to Gerry. I never knew if he meant half of it or not. He is a complex character, to say the least. When he's good he's very, very good, but he gets black moods. A year ago, I saw him for the first time in ages in a curry house in the East End, which I'd introduced him to years before. He came in with a woman and didn't speak. He looked at me, grunted, 'Ugh!' and sat down. Another time he might say, 'Oh! Malcolm! Hello, how are you?'

Sometimes, he'd do a really good show and come off stage in a horrible black mood. Another time he'd have one of the worst audiences ever and he'd come off and be as happy as anything. I think he hates success. Sometimes I had to pull him out of cars and on to the stage. He often refused to go on and his later agents, Avalon, had the same problems with him.

Once, in Edinburgh, he was asked to perform for five minutes on *Pick of the Fringe* on BBC TV Scotland. Michael Leggo was directing it – I hadn't met him since we were childhood neighbours in Lewisham. When I turned up, Arnold Brown was remonstrating with Gerry, who was refusing to go on. We cajoled him and threatened him and, in the end, he agreed to do it but only if he could do what he wanted because he was obviously going to be heavily censored. They filmed his act with the cunts and fucks and edited it with beeps. The result was like watching Gerry Sadowitz but listening to Morse code. The first year I took him up to Edinburgh, his advert in the Fringe programme read something like: 'Gerry Sadowitz – Glaswegian comic magician. A man who's had his act completely ripped off by Bing Hitler.' Bing Hitler was Craig Ferguson's stage name.

Craig Ferguson was in Edinburgh, represented by the high-powered Vivienne Clore, who later became my agent. He wanted to sue the Fringe Society and Gerry for libel, which meant I would be sued too because I had placed the advert. As I dug deeper into Gerry's accusation, I couldn't find one example where Craig Ferguson had nicked a line.

Gerry and Craig had started out at around the same time at the Tron Theatre in Glasgow when Craig was doing witty songs on the guitar. Possibly he was influenced by Gerry's style but that was as near as it got. He had a record out as Bing Hitler and there wasn't one line of Gerry's on it. He would have won his case but in the end the Fringe Society fined Gerry and he didn't get his ticket money, which upset him. It must have been worth about fifteen hundred pounds.

I arranged a meeting between the pair at which Craig said he hadn't pursued the case for the money and agreed to give it to a charity of Gerry's choice.

I took Gerry up to the Edinburgh Fringe twice. He hates Edinburgh because he's a Glaswegian. Or, at least, he sounds Glaswegian. He was actually born in America and has an American passport. His dad was an American who split up from Gerry's Glaswegian mother. Gerry came to Glasgow when he was very young and later said he had hardly any schooling because of a serious medical condition, which he insisted was coprophilia. He spent a lot of time in hospital, which is where he started to learn magic. He's written books on magic and writes for a monthly magic magazine about new tricks he's invented. Clever fellow.

He was a difficult artist to handle but I stayed with him because he was so good and everyone wanted him – the phone didn't stop ringing. Much of the time he wouldn't take the work but he wasn't consistent. One day he'd turn down a booking because he wasn't offered enough money, the next day he'd travel the length of the country for next to nothing. Once, before he'd become high-profile, I had a phone call from Sheffield University who were offering him three hundred pounds for a show, which was good money – most comics would go out for a hundred. Gerry asked if it included travel or accommodation, and when he was told it was an all-in fee he said no.

A couple of hours later, Sheffield Polytechnic offered him two hundred pounds plus travel and accommodation, which would add up to forty or fifty pounds. I phoned him and he said, 'I'll do it!'

The amount of his fee wasn't the most important thing to Gerry. I reckon they could have offered him three thousand and he'd have turned it down if it meant he had to get on that train and fork out cash for his own ticket and sort out a hotel. Small amounts of money seem to mean more to him than large sums. At one point in his career he was earning a lot – six thousand for one Avalon gig at the Clapham Grand. He was paid in cash and was driving home with the fellow from Avalon when the car broke down. The guy asked Gerry if he'd lend him the twelve pound cab fare to get home and Gerry refused. He had six thousand pounds in his pocket but it was the twelve pounds that seemed like a lot of money to Gerry.

A male-oriented comedian, much of Gerry's material was deliberately misogynistic. He once told me he wanted to play to an audience full of men and I said he probably *would* if he ended up in the nick. He wanted to fill Wembley Stadium with men, and do a show where the audience didn't pay to get in, just brought him presents. I thought *that* was quite a good idea.

People were always willing to book Gerry in live venues but TV was a different matter. Eventually he got his own TV series, but it didn't work. The point of Gerry's act was its shock and outrage value, which he couldn't provide on TV – or not to the level he did on stage.

Recently I heard that he is working as a shop assistant in a magic shop and still living with his mum in a council flat. He has had a series of agents and managers since me, but has never been as good as his days at the old Tunnel club, before his self-destructive ways blacked his career.

When we had started the Tunnel, we had received a three-thousand-pound grant from Greenwich Council to help set it up. (I bought a car with the money.) I had told them the Tunnel was going to bring art to the community. And it did. When the Council people came to check, I had a woman on the bill called Lilly Wicked. You couldn't find anyone more deserving of a Council grant: she was a female, black, a single parent, a lesbian and that week she'd broken her leg. She could have limped past the council offices and they would have thrown money out of the window at her. But Greenwich did OK from their grant. Through my agency, Tunnel Arts, I supplied them cheaply with lots of acts for the Greenwich Festival.

In 1987, I put up a tent on Blackheath. From my old hippie-festival days, I knew some people in Cornwall who had one for hire really cheap and we put on Harry Enfield, Gerry Sadowitz and Jools Holland. Greenwich Festival took the credit. When Jools performed, the tent was packed because he's a talented local lad.

I was in the 'dressing room', at the back of the tent, when Jools's mum came in and said, 'We can't get any tickets. They're sold out. Can we get in on the guest list?'

There was no guest list, but I sneaked seventeen people in. Bob Jones from the Council spotted me doing it and went mad. He didn't speak to me for years – but I couldn't have turned away Jools Holland's mum and his relatives. The show had sold out anyway, so the Council didn't lose money by it. It was Bob Jones who had driven me to the hospital when Frank was born. Recently he moved to a house near mine and I've gone round with the kids a couple of times and knocked on the door, but he's never let me in.

The Tunnel had an atmosphere of its own and was known for

its 'hard' audience who didn't suffer fools gladly and easily resorted to heckling. In certain circles it was referred to as the Glasgow Empire of the South: the audience at the Glasgow Empire hated southerners but at the Tunnel, they hated everyone. One double-act suffered from the start: they'd put on Red Indian head-dresses and were about to start beating their bongos when someone shouted, 'Oi! Malcolm! There's a couple of tropical fish on stage!'

The comedian Jim Tavare's first appearance was at the Tunnel. He's good now, but he wasn't always. He came on, stood in the middle of the stage, and said, 'Good evening, ladies and gentlemen. My name is Jim Tavare and I'm a schizophrenic.'

Immediately, someone yelled, 'Why don't you both fuck off, then?'

A Welsh comic called Noel James tried an act that involved painting his face and hands blue to give the impression he was blue all over. When I saw him in the dressing room, I thought he was going to go out and say he was a blue comic. But he didn't. He just talked bollocks for about thirty seconds until someone bellowed, 'Oi! Fuck off, you Smurf!' And he did. He never painted himself blue again.

Les Bubb is a mime artist. I think mime is a tragic waste of time, but *he's* very good. He blew up an invisible balloon, then played with an invisible rope, and did the hands-on-glass routine. After about ten minutes, he started to get a bit arty with his mimes until someone lost patience and shouted, 'Oi! For fuck's sake tell us a joke. I'm blind!' So he did. That's where he went wrong again: he was good at mime but no good at telling jokes. After a few seconds, the same fellow came back with, 'Oi, mate! Carry on with the mime! I'm deaf too!'

The Tunnel was soon successful so, from 1986, I decided to take the idea to the Edinburgh Festival. I called the show *Aaaaaaaaaargh!* because with all those As I'd get first place in the Fringe programme. Once, I had to have twenty-six As, because someone tried to sneak in with the Aaaaaaaaaaaaaardvark Theatre Company. One year, we were playing at the Pleasance. All the other shows on there had been reviewed by *The Scotsman* but we were 'wrong side of the tracks'. I thought I'd write my own review for them.

I bought a copy of the newspaper and picked out a reviewer's name at random – William Cook. I talked to someone I knew who used to write reviews for *The Scotsman* and found out how to do it. All you do is type it out double-spaced. That's the trick. Then, with Arthur Smith, I wrote a review of my own show, put William Cook's name at the bottom, folded it up, put it in an envelope and delivered it to the offices when all the staff had gone home. Sure enough, next day they printed it and after that the show was full up. *The Scotsman* went mad when they found out what I'd done and William Cook wouldn't speak to me for years – I don't know why, I presume he got paid for it.

There's one thing about Edinburgh that I forget every year until I arrive: audiences tend just to sit and look at you. They don't react. I don't know what it is. Maybe it's because they're just 'Edinburgh Festivalgoers'. It's not that they are surprised or shocked by *my* act – I've seen it with others too who go down a storm elsewhere. I've had audiences stare blankly at me for two weeks in Edinburgh, then I've come back to London on the Sunday Night, done Up the Creek and they've showed they enjoyed me.

Edinburgh audiences don't heckle but the sitting and staring can be worse. Heckling can be either creative or destructive. I had comedian Keith Allen heckle me at the Glastonbury Festival the year he'd been in the nick for a week for smashing a mirror at the Zanzibar club. He is a big fan of the Greatest Show on Legs and used to come along to a lot of our shows. I think it's wrong for one performer to heckle another, but Keith was good-spirited. I've only once heckled someone, at a miners' benefit in Peckham

151

Civic Centre. A man got up and did Mark Miwurdz's – he's now Mark Hurst – entire act, reading it off a bit of paper. He pretended he'd written it himself. I shouted, 'Oi! That's Mark Miwurdz's!' The audience looked at me as if I was mad and I was thrown out.

At the Tunnel, the main heckling was saved for the Open Spot, where people who perhaps hadn't been on stage before were trying out material. It never fails to amaze me how many people are keen to do this. I still get about ten calls a week from people wanting to do an Open Spot, people like Madame Poulet and Her Singing Chicken.

I booked Madame Poulet over the phone and, when she arrived, she tried to convince me she was Madame Edith and that Madame Poulet would arrive later. She left the 'chicken' in my office under a cloth, which I lifted when she wasn't there. It was a fake made of chicken feathers, some of which were painted pink. The Barbara Cartland of the chicken world.

In her act, she had a little triangular screen on stage, about waist height, so she could kneel behind it. That night, I announced, 'Ladies and gentlemen, will you please welcome Madame Poulet and her Singing Chicken . . .' And Madame Edith walked on, in her Madame Poulet disguise, wearing a hat with a black veil over her face. She knelt behind the screen, the chicken appeared over the top and Madame Poulet sang 'Je ne regrette rien' completely straight, in her own voice, with the chicken miming to it. This went on for about five minutes until she was interrupted by a few characters at the back: 'Cluck-cluck . . . cluck-cluck . . . cluck off!' Madame Poulet *almost* flew off the stage, left the club without saying a word, and I've never seen her since.

The best Open Spot I ever saw at the Tunnel was Phil Cool. It was his first alternative comedy gig in London. The worst, I think, was the Tapdancing Swede, who had the most piercing blue eyes I've ever seen. Unfortunately the stage at the Tunnel was the only area in the club that was fully carpeted. The Swede came on

152

wearing tails and looking immaculate clutching his backing-tape. He danced – silently – until the audience roared, 'Cab for the Swede!' and off he went. To this day, when an act is doing badly, people shout, 'Bring back the Swede!'

I've never been heckled seriously at the Tunnel, although there was one week when I was so bad I told the audience to heckle me off. The hecklers weren't always the same people, but there were some regulars – like the Pirate, who wore a blue handkerchief on his head with a knot in the back. Someone told me he worked in the stock market. He had a booming, Shakespearian-type voice and occasionally used to shout sarcastically, 'Larf-o-larf-o-larf!'

I wrote a script once with a woman who used to come to the Tunnel. It was an idea for a TV sitcom to be called *Hellfire and Hecklers*, set in a club with backstage goings-on. Something similar called *Packet of Three* was done on Channel 4 a couple of years later but ours was never taken up – perhaps because it wasn't very good.

I used to talk to some of the Tunnel hecklers after a show but I never openly encouraged them. In fact, I wrote notices which I left on the tables pointing out that the heckling was getting a bit too much. But then they heckled the notices. When they finally realised that they were going too far they hummed the acts off instead.

The heckling issue eventually came to a head one night when I was in Edinburgh and 'Clarence and Joy Pickles' (Adam Wide and Babs Sutton from the old National Revue Company) appeared doing a parody of an old music-hall couple. No longer content with verbal abuse, the hecklers armed themselves with various missiles which they flung at the stage. Babs was hit between the eyes with a glass, which broke her spectacles.

Arthur Smith was the headline act, appearing at the end of the show. He started his act and – he's a very good performer – was going down well with the audience. After five minutes, though,

153

he stopped dead, said, '*They* are friends of mine. *You* are all animals,' and walked off stage.

The Babs incident was the beginning of the end for the Tunnel. It eventually closed because the landlord decided to put on acid house raves every Saturday night and the police raided it. They closed off the Blackwall Tunnel and hid in there, helicoptered in the reserves, then flooded into the pub through skylights, windows and doors. There were about three hundred kids in the pub at four in the morning – all quite legal, because the landlord wasn't selling alcohol. The police search yielded only thirty quid's worth of dope found in one woman's handbag, from an operation that reputedly cost around a quarter of a million – which seriously upset the Old Bill. Next time the landlord applied for his licence, he was turned down, and it wasn't until 1995 that new management got it back.

There was nothing memorable about the last night of the Tunnel because I didn't know it was going to be the last night. We ran Sunday Night at the Tunnel Palladium as normal. On the following Saturday the Mitre was raided and closed.

In 1988 Pip became pregnant again. Between pregnancies, I had left her and Frank a couple of times and gone to live at the Tunnel. She had left me once – she had an affair with someone called Dave, who phoned me the other day trying to sell me a car.

Pip had wanted to have the second baby at home but a few weeks before it was due her blood pressure soared and she had to go into hospital. The doctors diagnosed pre-eclampsia, which can be fatal, and decided to induce the baby.

That day, 7 December, the hospital was busy, and all the delivery rooms were full so Pip was put into a little side ward. She was having contractions and I tried to get nurses to come to her but they were all too busy.

My daughter Poppy was born in this little side ward at 11.05

154

– a bad time for me because the pubs had closed. After the birth a midwife insisted Pip had an injection to speed up the delivery of the afterbirth. Pip didn't want the injection but she was so weak that she went along with it. I said goodbye to her at about 11.30, because she looked so tired, went home and had a drink with Jools Holland, who lived opposite.

The next day, Frank and I went in to see her and Poppy but she sent us away because she didn't feel well. Later that day, in the run-up to Christmas, I did a rare afternoon show at a college in Bromley. When I got home afterwards, Pip's mother was waiting for me. The intensive care unit at Greenwich Hospital had phoned and Pip was seriously ill. I went straight there to be greeted by a doctor who told me she was probably going to die.

I went into her room to find her comatose and attached to all sorts of machines. Worse, her liver and kidneys had packed up. Next day, she was taken by ambulance with a police escort to Dulwich Hospital, which has a kidney unit. Her mother drove me there and nearly killed us about three times because, understandably, she was in such a panic. At Dulwich, we found lots of top surgeons rushing around looking panicky too. Something had gone wrong.

Pip was in a coma for about a week, during which I lived at the hospital. Her dad came up from Bournemouth in tears and her mum was in a terrible state. Chris Lynam was great: he came to stay at the hospital with me. Eventually, Pip came round but her kidneys still weren't working and for a time she was on dialysis. I took Poppy home and looked after her until Pip was allowed to leave hospital just after Christmas. She still wasn't well, so for the next two or three months the responsibility for our new baby mostly fell on me – bottle of milk in one hand, fag in the other.

Luckily, Pip made an almost full recovery, with 90 per cent of her kidney function, and sued Greenwich Hospital. They settled out of court. She also decided, not surprisingly after all she'd been through, that she would be sterilised. When she went back in, the surgeons found a massive non-malignant tumour in her womb which they removed. That was worrying too, at the time, but now I make jokes about it, of course.

For part of the time Pip was in hospital her mother came to help out with Poppy and occupied the main bedroom on the first floor. She is a Justice of the Peace in Bournemouth – and one of the cleanest women you could meet. She practically polished the inside of our wastebin.

One night, I went down to the pub, got a bit drunk and met one of the Hell's Angels who had the garage at the back of the Tunnel. He's constantly covered in grease because he works with cars and bikes and goes straight from work into the pub. Tattoos, long hair with grease dripping off it. When we were talking, I realised I had forgotten my front-door key. I said, 'I can't knock up the mother-in-law. She'll go bloody mad!'

'I'll get you in,' he said, 'I used to do a bit of burglary.'

I thought, Between us we should be all right.

We drove back to my house in his beaten-up old Vauxhall Cresta. I went across to Jools Holland's house and borrowed some ladders I knew he kept in his side alley. We decided to climb in the front window of the room where my mother-in-law was sleeping. The Hell's Angel went up first, prised open the window and put his head through, about six feet from where her face rested on the pillow. We discovered she was a light sleeper . . .

She went home the next day and left me to look after Poppy on my own.

CHAPTER 10

A FIREWORK UP THE BUM

After the Tunnel closed, agent Addison Cresswell set up a similar enterprise at the Albany Empire on Sunday nights. He asked me to compère it for a month because I was popular locally. Each gig was incident packed and I only lasted three weeks.

On the first Sunday, we put on a young comic called Alex Langdon. He was about fifteen and his dad, John Langdon, wrote for *Punch*. The lad's script had been written for him by his dad so a man's words were coming out of a boy's mouth. There was something a bit sad about that and especially because Alex 'died'.

I said to the audience, 'Well, he was shit but he's still young.' What I didn't know when I said this was that he was sitting crying at the side of the stage. At the interval, I came off and found him in floods of tears. I felt like a rat.

The next week, we had a double-act which wasn't much appreciated by the audience. Before they went off, this quick-thinking duo said, 'Don't throw your beer glasses at us. Throw them at Malcolm when he comes back on.' And they did.

On the third Sunday, I was in the middle of my act and was dying for a piss so I did it on the stage. It wasn't gratuitous or that I just fancied a piss: someone shouted something at me and one thing led to another. It was at the back of the stage, only a little one, and I cleaned it up afterwards. But I was sacked as compère and replaced by Jack Dee.

Part of the problem that night was that the people who financed the Albany were in the audience, as was Teddy Kennedy, the then artistic director. He was an American and, perhaps, had no sense of irony. The people who had handed out the grant didn't think my pissing was entertaining either. Nobody's perfect.

I also had trouble at the Zap club in Brighton. It was a great place, under some arches on the beach, and it had been expanded so that there was space for cabaret. I pissed on stage here too.

Again, I reckoned it was called for although I can't remember now which line led up to it. The Zap's cabaret evenings stopped soon afterwards.

I've done thousands of shows and I've only pissed on stage three times – well, maybe four. That's not a lot. The first time I did it was at the Tunnel. A man was sitting in the front row, hideously drunk. So drunk, in fact, that he had fallen asleep and was snoring loudly through all the acts. We didn't have bouncers at the Tunnel but he couldn't have been thrown out anyway, because he was right at the front and right in the middle. At the end of the show, I said to the audience, 'I've been dying for a piss. I don't know whether to go to the toilet or go on him.'

'Go on him!' they yelled.

I pissed on his head – and he slept through it.

At the end of the night, he must have woken up and left but I didn't see him go. He was back the next week – he was quite a big bloke – and he came up to me as if he was about to hit me. He said, 'You pissed on my head last week, didn't you?'

I said, 'Yes. Sorry about that.'

'No problem,' he said. 'People have been talking about it all week. It's been great.' And he shook my hand.

I normally go to the toilet before I get on stage but certain things happen on certain nights and you need to do something either to get the audience on your side or out of their stupor. A bit of a shock is what's needed and pissing is the liquid equivalent of swearing.

Sometimes, when things are really desperate – or even when the act has gone down particularly well – I do an impression of General de Gaulle. Martin Soan started that one. You have to be naked, of course. If Martin and I do the impression together, I take off my spectacles and hold them at the top of his knob. For some reason, anyone's knob looks like General de Gaulle's nose. (Try it yourselves, gents.) Then we get the audience singing the

159

French national anthem and off we go. I found out how to do this from one of Spike Milligan's autobiographical books. There was a bit where a guy did all sorts of impressions with his testicles and his knob, including two eggs on a plate with a sausage. And General de Gaulle. The Tunnel audience always liked it.

Chris Lynam was one of the most popular acts with any Tunnel audience that enjoyed General de Gaulle. He had been in the Greatest Show on Legs at one point. One day we were wondering how to follow the Balloon Dance. We would all be naked and unless we thought of something we'd just have to walk off stage, which, we agreed, was no way to finish the act. 'Well,' I said, 'you might as well stick a banger up your arse!'

'Good idea!' Chris said. 'You do it!'

So I was the first one to do it but I only did it once. You don't stick the banger *up* your arse, you clench it between your buttocks, then light it. But I didn't have the necessary muscle-control and the banger drooped, setting light to the hairs on my testicles. I said to Chris, 'You'd better do it.'

Now his act ends with him sticking a firework up his bum, to the accompaniment of 'There's No Business Like Show Business'. The firework is lit and he exits the stage trailing glorious sparks. Sometimes it's a three-stage Roman Candle shooting forth increasingly spectacular jets of silver sparkles. Good finish. Difficult to follow.

The first year he did it in Edinburgh, we were playing a little pub called the Comedy Boom. The Banger-up-the-Bum routine was passed by the fire officer, whose name was Maurice Gibb. (No, not the Bee-Gee.) We did it the first night but the landlord said, 'You're not doing *that* in *my* pub!'

I told him we'd compromise. At the end of our show, we'd take the audience outside and do it in the street. On the second night that's what we did and it wasn't just the audience from the show who were there: it drew a bit of a crowd.

The landlord said, 'No! You're not doing that again. It's bringing my pub into disrepute.' So we videoed the routine and showed the film to the audience, but it wasn't the same.

On the last night of our run, I decided we'd do it again for real. We'd been paid already, so fuck the landlord. And we'd had other rows with him about our act.

Chris bought an extra-large firework. That night – banger in the bottom – lit – 'No Business Like Show Business' – and it set the pub alight. Just the wall. A bit of plaster. It wasn't much damage. But some people . . . moan, moan, moan.

The next year, the Greatest Show on Legs played the Assembly Rooms, *the* prestige venue at the Edinburgh Fringe. Same thing again. The fire officer passed it. First night went without a hitch. Lovely. On the second night, it set off the fire alarms and the entire building was evacuated – about three thousand people had to get out, including our audience and some Russians who were doing a four-hour play and had only three minutes to go.

We were all standing around outside the Assembly Rooms when the fire engines turned up with Maurice Gibb, ready with his hose. When he saw me naked and Chris Lyñam, the penny dropped. 'Banger up the bum?' he enquired.

'Yes,' I said.

'Hoses away, lads!' he said. And off they went.

The Russians went back upstairs and did the last three minutes of their play.

Chris Luby was always popular both at the Tunnel and in Edinburgh. We had met when we were both in *The Mad Show*. His act was – and still is – oral impressions. He can do wartime aeroplanes, racing cars and the entire Trooping the Colour ceremony, plus machines, drums and military people.' His act lasts twenty minutes and he's made a good living out of it.

On stage, he has a military air, a bit Air Force, maybe, but he was never in the RAF. When I met him, he had been a civil

161

servant for fifteen years. A real boring, pen-pushing job. He lived on a council estate in Bromley, South East London. At the time, he didn't have a car, so I used to give him a lift home after *The Mad Show*. Every night followed the same pattern. I would start the engine and he would say: 'Chocks away!' Then he'd be in first gear, changing up until we got to the first bend when his tyres screeched and he'd yell, 'Bank left! Bank left!' It was the same every night for three months and I didn't hit him one. On one journey back from Manchester, after twenty minutes of Chris's sound effects, Arthur Smith gave him fifty pounds to keep quiet. It's a talented act, but limited.

Chris was in the Falklands just before the conflict broke out, and he was in Saudi Arabia, entertaining the troops, at the outset of the Gulf War. He could have made a fortune travelling round Army and RAF bases during the Cold War. But the night I thought his career might not be a runaway success was when I saw him drunk at the Comedy Store.

Wizo was running a 'Fun Bus', a double-decker sponsored by a lager company. During the summer, he got comics to perform on it and told them they could do whatever they liked. They could even tell the driver where to go or take the audience off the bus. When he booked me for a week I took Chris Luby along.

The bus was parked near the Aldwych and Chris soon had the audience drilling in the street. He'd have made a great sergeant-major: 'Stand by the left! Quick march!' and off they went. The bus turned into an aeroplane when we got back on. 'Fasten your seat-belts!' roared Chris, slipping into his Second World War bomber.

We drove down to the Montague Arms in New Cross where a talent competition was being held. I entered playing the mouth organ, but I don't know if I won or not because we had to go back into town. During the journey Chris was drinking the lager laid on by the sponsors and when we dropped off the bus he wanted to carry on, so we went to the Comedy Store, where he proceeded to get legless until he was asked to leave.

It was about two in the morning and I was a bit drunk too but not as bad as Chris. After some discussion we staggered down to Charing Cross and caught the N77 to Greenwich. Chris couldn't get upstairs, but I did and was sitting quietly minding my own business waiting for the bus to leave when I heard: 'Engage thrust! Bank left! Chocks away!' and we were back in the bomber.

After about half an hour of it, the driver and passengers could take no more. We stopped briefly at New Cross and I watched Chris being thrown out of the bus. As we pulled away, he was lying flat on the pavement. New Cross is about two miles from where he lived.

The next morning I phoned his wife to find out what had happened to him. She didn't know but told me he had given a cab driver a cheque for eighty-three pounds.

When I was an agent, I had Chris for a while as a client. I've done that sort of work mostly to help people along the way rather than to make money out of them. I took on Chris and Gerry Sadowitz because I thought they were good. When I first started agenting out of the Tunnel, I was one of the few people working with alternative acts and I liked the idea of having another string to my bow. I'm currently representing Ricky Grover and the Bastard Son of Tommy Cooper, and I used to look after Charlie Chuck. He's a good bloke – when he came into a bit of money, he sent me a large cheque in gratitude for my help.

Gerry Sadowitz was the opposite. He phoned me up a couple of Christmases ago and said I owed him £2000 because I never got him enough work when I was his agent. Nothing could be further from the truth: he didn't want to do most of it.

I also agented for female ventriloquist Terri Rogers and took her up to Edinburgh several times. She says she's fifty-odd but I think she's a bit more than that. One year, I wanted her to fake a heart attack and 'die' on stage. My fireman friend Maurice Gibb was lined up to come on stage and carry off the body. I planned a benefit in her memory, at the end of which, I was going to say: 'Ladies and gentlemen, will you please welcome Terri Rogers.' And on she'd walk. But she wouldn't do it.

Terri used to do the show, come back, have a cup of tea and go to bed. But during one Edinburgh run one of the other performers, Angry Young Accordionist John Moloney, was having a relationship with a girl. They were coming back late and making 'noises'. After about a week of all this shagging in the room next to hers, I found Terry one morning lying face-down across the kitchen table, crying and kicking her legs saying: 'I can't go on! I can't go on!'

She hates being thought of as elderly. A reviewer once called her 'the brilliant 70-year-old ventriloquist'. She turned up the next night, cases packed, quivering with rage, saying, 'I'm going home.' But she didn't.

CHAPTER 11

THE WONDERFUL WORLD OF
TELEVISION

In 1989, I was doing my show in Edinburgh with Chris Luby and Terri Rogers when Noel Gay Television were contracted to make entertainment programmes for the new BSB satellite channels. One of their planned programmes was a rip-off of the bizarre American talent series *The Gong Show*, from which the idea for the Comedy Store's gong had arisen.

Two Noel Gay producers saw me in Edinburgh, then took me out for the traditional Media Meal in London. They asked if I had anything shady in my past. I said, 'No,' and they asked me to host what was then called *The Cockroach Show*. It was to be a series of sixty-five half-hour programmes after the style of *The Gong Show*. The money wasn't so good – five hundred pounds per show, not Cilla Black megabucks – but it could have been worse. I claimed a researcher's fee too because they had to find all these weird acts. That was another five hundred a week.

I went round the country auditioning acts with Cecil Korer, the producer of *The Cockroach Show* pilot, and some glamorous girl he had with him. (One of Cecil's proudest claims to fame was as producer of the appalling 1980s Channel 4 series *Mini-Pops*.) Some of the acts we saw were indescribably bizarre. You had to be there. But in the end, we selected enough for two pilots: *The Flip Show*, which had hand-held hooters instead of a gong, and *Pull the Plug!* in which lights were turned off progressively until the act was in darkness and had to stop. We recorded the shows in Gillingham with Jools Holland, Cardew Robinson and Ned Sherrin on the panel. Cardew had been a judge years back at Mr Looniverse on *The Mad Show*. In spite of all our efforts, though, the pilots were never taken up by BSB. We were never told exactly why.

By 1989, Wizo – following his non-career as a performer – had decided he too should become an agent. He had been working as stage manager at the Tramshed and he knew Addison Cresswell, who was agent for people like Skint Video, Jeremy Hardy and Mark Thomas. They were all disillusioned with Addison and Wizo just nicked the lot off him. He formed a co-operative with them all, called it Stage Left and did quite well for maybe three years. Most of his acts featured in the Noel Gay/BSB shows.

When I started working for Noel Gay Television, Gerry Sadowitz and I had an amicable parting of the ways. With the Noel Gay work, I couldn't devote all my time to managing Gerry – which he needed. So my choice was either to join forces with the then fledgling Avalon agency or just hand Gerry over to them totally, which is what happened.

And it was while I was working for Noel Gay that I met Charlie Chuck. I auditioned him for the Gillingham pilots, although he did not appear on them. When I finished with Noel Gay, I decided to go back into management and become something between an agent and a manager for Charlie, whose act is *very* bizarre. It consists of a sequence of non-sequiturs. In those days, he started by smashing an entire drum kit to bits, then saying, 'Ey an beway, flippin de bow-wow . . . Donkey! Woof-bark . . . Donkey! . . . Woof-bark . . . Donkey . . . Eee-aw. Eee-aw. Eee-aw.' You get the picture. He told me that he'd borrowed – borrowed! – the drum kit from a music shop round the corner.

The day I auditioned him in Nottingham, he was there with seven or eight mainstream types who were with their agents. The others were doing impressions of Norman Wisdom and Michael Crawford as Frank Spencer in *Some Mothers Do 'Ave 'Em* – things anyone had seen a million times before. Then came Charlie Chuck with his drum kit. He played it, destroyed it and the agents all sat up agog and aghast. They should have signed him up there and then, because the others weren't going to get anywhere. Or perhaps they did. Perhaps they're playing cruise liners.

It's not only difficult to describe Charlie's act, it's impossible to describe *him*. He's fifty and looks like a seventies-reject: a

167

haggard and demented pixie who's just had fifty thousand volts put through him because his curly hair stands out like that of a latter-day white Jimi Hendrix. He looks quite different off-stage. He toured Europe for ten years as drummer with the Amazing Bavarian Stompers and discovered alternative stand-up relatively late in life. He plays summer seasons in Great Yarmouth and does Reeves and Mortimer tours, to totally different audiences but with equal ease. His mainstream audiences don't understand most of what they're watching, though. Charlie Chuck was and is unique. An original.

People wonder if he is mad off-stage too, but he's a normal sort of fellow. His real name is Dave, he lives in a nice little house near Leicester, he's married with children and he's a Christian. He was easy for me to work with as his agent. He'd do more or less any gig offered to him, he was always there on time and he didn't get drunk.

My only problem with Charlie Chuck was that whenever I advised him on his act, he did exactly the opposite. In the end, I suggested the opposite of what I thought he should do but some sixth sense alerted him and he carried on in his own way as usual. Sometimes, for instance, if he's panicking a bit, he'll tell 'Doctor, Doctor' jokes, which I don't think he should bother with. But he tells them even if the surreal stuff is going down well, which can throw the whole act out.

I never knew what he was going to do when he went on stage. Perhaps neither did he. He usually started by wrecking a drum kit – but not always. His act *has* changed over the years, but not much. It wasn't a difficult act to sell to bookers because, by then, people had grown to trust my judgement. What is difficult – can be almost impossible – is trying to get across what an act is about unless it's obviously spectacular, swallowing rabbits, for instance. Years before, I had tried to get Arabella Churchill, of the Glastonbury Festival, to book Harry Enfield. She said, 'What does he do?'

168

'He does all these characters,' I said. 'One of them's a Greek character called Stavros and another one's a posh character and he's extremely funny.'

She'd never seen him, so she didn't book him. She was kicking herself the next year. As I've said before, with some acts, you've got to have been there.

Charlie Chuck appeared with me on a TV pilot: a cross between a game show and a variety show I thought up for Noel Gay. I went to see Channel 4's commissioning editor for entertainment, Seamus Cassidy, to talk about it. The game show side was to be called *Lose Yer Shirt!* and if the contestants got the answers wrong, they would lose their own property. Their washing machine would be smashed up in front of them. Seamus liked the sound of it and *Lose Yer Shirt!* was to take place in the middle of a variety show called *Hardee's Half Hour*. The pilot was made, in Gillingham again, and again it was never taken up. Again I don't know why.

It was around this time that I started up a Last Friday in the Month comedy club in Suffolk. One of the Box Brothers – Paul Fitzgerald – lives in a small village near Bungay with a nice pub called the King's Head, which has an ideal space for comedy. I had played there with the Greatest Show on Legs. The first evening was well attended, but it gradually went downhill. Too cosmopolitan for them, I think. An Oxbridge classical-music duo, called Miles and Millner, did well there and so did Chris Luby. They loved Miles and Millner because the act was sketches involving music to which anyone could relate, and Chris Luby's act is mad enough to appeal across the board anywhere (once).

One night, Chris Luby, Mark Hurst and Brenda Gilhooley (now known as Gayle Tuesday) were all booked to appear at the King's Head. They drove over separately from me because I had already gone up with Pip for the weekend. Paul Fitzgerald was going to give us all a meal before the gig. I told Chris to telephone when he arrived at the pub and I'd give him directions to Paul's cottage. He rang at around five-thirty and I gave him instructions for the six-mile drive.

At six-thirty the meal was ready. No sign of Luby.

Seven-thirty. No sign of Luby.

The gig was due to start at eight.

Eight o'clock. No sign of Luby.

We went off to the gig. On the way, we found him. Between the pub and the cottage, Chris had spotted a private aeroplane museum in the back garden of another pub. He was in heaven. He had aeroplanes and alcohol – and we had to drag him to the gig.

The King's Head is one of those old-fashioned pubs with a courtyard where they used to put the coaches. The landlord had about five kids, ranging from about seven to twelve. After the gig, at about midnight, I happened to glance out of a window to see Chris Luby drilling the kids. They had broomsticks over their shoulders and were marching round the courtyard to his commands: 'Eyes right! Quick march!'

The most enjoyable TV I've done were my *Comic Strip* films. In the first, I was a builder. Then I became a policeman and I had to drive a police car up to someone's house – I was banned at the time but I hadn't told the producers so I got to race down these streets in Streatham. Until a genuine police car stopped me. Luckily for me, I got away with it.

The best of the *Comic Strip* films, as far as I was concerned, was *The Yob*, filmed just round the corner from my house and in which I played a ticket inspector. I got up that morning, put on a uniform and walked 150 yards to the Greenwich foot tunnel, which had been dressed up to look like a tube station. My lines were, 'Tickets, please! O, you! Tickets, please!' Then an old lady kneed me in the groin and that was it. We did it in two takes and I was away by ten with six hundred pounds in my pocket.

In *GLC*, another *Comic Strip* film, I was Beefeater Two to

Keith Allen's Beefeater One. At the time I was in Edinburgh and it was to be filmed in London in a house in my road. I flew down from Edinburgh, did a day's filming in my own road, then flew back to Edinburgh for the evening performance. ·

To me, it's not the quality of the part that's important, it's how far I have to travel and how easy it is.

I appeared in the first series of *Blackadder* for about thirty seconds as an Egyptian. The Greatest Show on Legs – which then included me, Martin Soan and Martin Clarke – were meant to be Egyptian mummers there to amuse the king. I was painted orange and couldn't wear my glasses. I recently met an American comic who is a big *Blackadder* fan. She took one look at me and said, 'Hey! You were the Egyptian!' I keep getting cheques for that appearance so I'm glad I did it. I got a whole batch the other day, including forty-seven pence for a screening in Greece and £2.17 for one in Croatia. Things must be looking up in Croatia.

One good thing about working for Noel Gay was that, in 1990, I found out about the annual *Just For Laughs* comedy festival in Montreal.

In London, Wizo had met a taxi driver who had somehow got him two return tickets to New York for fifty pounds each. He said to me, 'Why don't we go over to Montreal via New York?' I was all for it so he sold me one ticket and left the next day.

I followed a week later. Or, at least, I tried to. When I got to the departure desk at Gatwick, I discovered I had a one-way ticket from New York to London. I was stuck. I'd arranged to meet a load of people in Montreal the next day so I had no alternative but to buy a ticket costing three hundred pounds from London to Montreal. The cheque bounced, but that's another matter.

When I arrived at the Delta Hotel in Montreal I said I was with Noel Gay. The company had a big group of people staying there, all of whom I had worked with in London, so everything was free for a week since they assumed they must be paying for me too. Wizo pulled the same stunt successfully although he'd never had actually worked for Noel Gay.

I was there as a TV person but I performed the Banger-up-the-Bum routine with Chris Lynam at the Club Soda – an event still talked about to this day.

Afterwards, Wizo and I had to go to New York so that I could use my cheap air ticket home; I did a bit of a stand-up there, but word had reached the show organisers about my Montreal performance and no one wanted to risk letting me go on stage. I did a small spot at a place called Caroline's, which went down well, but the Americans are surprisingly cautious. When Chris Lynam was in New York a week later, though, he did the Banger-up-the-Bum, with full permission, at Caroline's club.

It was on this trip that Wizo demonstrated his talent for re-inventing himself. Montreal set him off because the Noel Gay bunch had been trying to impress each other with how important they all were. Wizo fell for it hook, line and sinker and I heard him telling someone he ran Noel Gay Television. By the time we got to New York, however, he had promoted himself and was explaining to this woman that he was chief executive of the BBC. She, being an American, believed him. He was only about thirty-five at the time.

I went to *Just For Laughs* again in 1992 and did the Balloon Dance with the Greatest Show on Legs. We went down better than any other British act, even though we weren't in the official British contingent sponsored by Channel 4. We had been invited by the festival organisers and even appeared on French television but not on Channel 4.

Although the audience liked our act, several American performers thought it was too simple – a bit of a con. American stand-ups spend hours perfecting each word, phrase and pause while we just came on stage naked and shuffled a few balloons about. Despite that we were nominated for, but didn't get, a

Gemini TV Award (the Canadian equivalent of the BAFTAs) as Best Performance on a Light Entertainment Programme.

During the festival I heard that the British Consul had invited the official British contingent to the Embassy. As we were British and we were there, I thought we shouldn't miss out on the party, so I gatecrashed it. At one point, I asked some fellow why he was there. He told me, 'I'm the Consul.' Whoops. Quick as a flash, I said, 'I had one of them but the gearbox went.' Nothing! Straight face. Mine was red.

The official British contingent in Montreal – Paul Merton, Jeremy Hardy *et al.* – were being courted by Hollywood producers but all the Greatest Show on Legs got was some sad German fellow called Achim Rhoder. He's a big agent – in more senses than one as he stands six foot six tall. He came over to us and said, 'We'd like you to perform at the Cologne Festival.'

So we did. The German TV audience likes to see people falling over so, in Germany, we perform sketches in which we do just that. Not known for their sense of humour, the Germans. There are Three Golden Rules of Comedy:

1. If in doubt, wobble about.

2. If that don't work, fall over.

3. If that don't work – knob out!

In Germany, we fall over a lot. A British comic called George Egg is a giant showbiz hero in Germany. He just does a basic juggling act and sticks a coat-hanger through his ear, but they love him. Germans like the straightforward street acts.

CHAPTER 12

ENGAGED TO JULIA, MARRIED TO JANE, SET UPON BY ANNIE THE GERMAN

The day the gravy train hit the buffers for me and a few others at Noel Gay was when Sky bought out BSB. It was 1990 and I started a new club in Greenwich called Up the Creek. It was going to be called Malcolm's, but someone told me that made it sound like it was in Essex, so I changed it.

I had been looking for something to replace the Tunnel and I chanced upon a building which had originally been a Seamen's Mission, then an Electric Cinema and most recently a snooker hall. Three brothers had bought the freehold in the 1980s, when the property boom was at its height, and had wanted to convert it into offices but discovered that it had to be used for leisure. An attempt to use it as a disco failed when the kids climbed over the roof into the pub next door, and after a half-hearted effort at turning it into a rave venue, nothing much happened there until the day I saw the sign. It read:

BUILDING FOR LEASE OR SALE

On the spot I decided that Wizo and I would rent it. Wizo, however, insisted we consult an accountant, who advised against it. Then I tried Jools Holland, but he was too involved with his studio. However, I had already shown my plans for a comedy club to the brothers who owned the building, and they said if I provided my expertise and could fill the place they'd give me one-third ownership.

One of my less well-known talents is a flair for publicity. I stood for Parliament again in the 1991 general election, putting up my own money. That way I was entitled to a free mail shot to all my potential constituents – about 42,000 people in Greenwich. I selected the addresses of people who might come to Up the Creek and sent flyers to about 10,000 people for nothing, which saved me around two and a half grand in postage alone – or, at any rate, two grand because I lost my five-hundred-pound election deposit.

Up the Creek was a success from its first night on Hallowe'en in 1990. The opening month featured all the big names: Squeeze came for the opening press night, and Jools Holland, Vic Reeves, Jo Brand, all the old chums turned out too. And the brothers, my business partners, have been very good to me.

Those three grew up in poverty in Bellingham, near Lewisham, fairly close to where I lived. Their grandfather owned a scrap-metal dealer's. When I was a kid there was a garden in the front of it where pebbles in the grass spelt out:

KING OF LEE

I used to think a real king lived there; it had been the brothers' grandfather. They started off selling gear-boxes, then went into 'computer-dating' before the big agencies were formed. Instead of finding true love for lonely hearts with a computer, though, they employed an old lady with index cards. It cost a fiver to join their agency and one brother told me Ford-Transit-loads of cash poured in every day. Thing was, though, this old lady was matching up Jews with Catholics, atheists with born-again Christians, eighty-year-old women with eighteen-year-old men . . .

One brother got into property, made a pile and bought a house in Hollywood next door to *Starsky and Hutch* star David Soul. He had a big boat, too, moored at St Katherine's Wharf by the Tower of London, *and* a Lear Jet.

177

The brothers are businessmen who've been bitten by the show-biz bug. When Up the Creek proved successful, they bought the old Willesden Empire in North West London and turned it into the Comedy Empire, ten times the size of Up the Creek. I was the promoter: we got good publicity and when we had Names on it was full – bursting at the seams when Jo Brand came – but it was in the wrong place and it was too big. I hated the journey to Willesden: it took me an hour to get there, whereas I can get from my house to Up the Creek in five minutes. And I know everyone round here: I go out my door and someone in the street will say, 'Hello, Malcolm!' Normally, of course, it's the bailiffs. But in Willesden I didn't know anyone and I don't really like having to be out of South East London.

I like routine and knowing where I am – I like to know that the chip shop opens at six o'clock. Sure I like travelling around but no way could I go away for a year. I'd miss coming to Up the Creek on a Sunday. I had to go to Australia for five weeks in 1994 and I missed home. When I was touring round the West Country in the 1970s I often came back to South East London and I always will. Part of the reason I split up with Pip was that she wanted to live in the country and almost persuaded me to buy a house in Norfolk. We spent three years together in Kent, but that was only thirty miles away and I must have spent three-quarters of that time in Greenwich. That village near Maidstone was too quiet for me and I couldn't sleep for the first week – no cars going past. Also I'm a night person, can't sleep anyway before one or two a.m. Where can you get a kebab at two in the morning in Stoke-sub-Normal? Country life is high on my list of things that sensible people shouldn't subscribe to. But Pip wanted an Old Country Cottage, which she now has with her new man. It would drive me up the bloody wall.

Another of my pet hates is a dinner party. What is a 'dinner party'? As far as I'm concerned the two don't go together. Dinner is dinner: you eat and then you go out. A party is a party: you don't eat anything. Like a 'walking holiday'. Walking is walking and a holiday is lying on the beach with a packet of fags.

My split with Pip in 1991 was amicable. We had been together thirteen years and we had just drifted apart. I left her and moved in with a flatmate called Julia, who had just separated from her husband Barry Keefe, the playwright who wrote the film *The Long Good Friday*. Our flat was at 1 Mell Street, Greenwich. It's probably the shortest street in the world as the only building in it is 1 Mell Street. The flat, which was undecorated, was above a shop selling paint, tiles and decorating materials. Devoted to South East London though I am, this was not a place I cherished and since it coincided with the first time that I had been single in years I spent most of my time on the blower to all the old flames I could muster. I had six months of sex and drugs and rock 'n' roll (I can't stand rock 'n' roll) including one week where I managed to copulate with eight different women (two on Sunday).

I had of course tried to shag Julia, too, but here I failed. She remained a flatmate but wasn't into mating. Or at least not with me. We did share many things, naturally; we even co-owned a long leather coat that she had bought but I decided looked much finer on me. And we often mooched around together. When I was asked to screen test for a part in the video recording of a live show in Newcastle of *Vic Reeves Big Night Out* Julia was keen to come along on the jaunt.

The day before we were to head North I had gone into Ladbroke's at Charing Cross with twenty pounds and in a miraculous series of drink-inspired bets had won five thousand two hundred pounds by the end of the afternoon. Ladbroke's didn't have enough cash in the office to pay me. I agreed to pick up my winnings the following day. For some reason Julia and I convinced ourselves that the most appropriate place for this vast booty was a hat box she intended to take to Newcastle. So we turned up at King's Cross

179

MALCOLM HARDEE

for the train, Julia manically clinging to her hat box and me feeling
like the cock of the walk as I swaggered along in the favourite
leather coat – though I probably looked more like a raddled Gestapo torturer.

In Newcastle we were booked into the five-star Copthorne
Hotel where Vic Reeves, Simon Day, Jimmy Nail and assorted
others connected with Vic's *Big Night Out* were staying. Julia and
I scanned our room for a hiding place for the five grand and the
only thing even vaguely suitable was a tall vase on top of the
television. I picked the vase up, shook it, and tipped out a pack
of very pornographic playing cards. There were pictures of people
– mainly – doing things even I wouldn't do. I pocketed the cards.
In case the owner came back in search of them we decided not to
put the cash in the vase and so it ended up divided between the
pockets of the leather coat.

I failed to make it on to Vic's video but the live show was
jolly. We trooped back from it on Vic's tour bus – a sort of mobile
hotel with bedrooms and lounge area – and spent a liquid evening in
the Copthorne bar. I was one of the last to leave and when I was
approaching my room I realised that Simon Day, who had been
chosen in preference to me for the video, was on the same landing.
He had been given the presidential suite – a very grand affair with
a balcony that ran along the front of the hotel. I suspected that Simon
had retired early to his room because he had lured some unsuspecting female there and, all things considered, it seemed right that
I should bid him a congratulatory goodnight.

Wearing only the leather coat and a pair of socks I crawled
along the balcony of my room and clambered across to Simon's.
I hammered on his window intending to flash open the coat when he
pulled back the curtains. Not a sound. Disappointed I eventually
returned to my room to find Julia in her bed, cowering under the
sheets, and two men with guns pointed at me. They were Special
Branch. Anti-terrorism. And I vaguely recalled some notices

180

pinned in the hotel about a senior politician – Michael Heseltine, I think – who was staying there and 'would guests behave accordingly' as the Special Branch boys handcuffed me and marched me down to a Portakabin in the car park that was both their headquarters and their prison cell.

I was asked to turn out my pockets: £5,200 in cash and a very pornographic pack of playing cards. I was asked for my address, which I gave as 1 Mell Street, Greenwich, which they ran through their computer. This told them a fact that I had known but not been unduly bothered by before: that Mell Street had been the home of Gerald Tuite, the convicted IRA bomber who had been arrested there some years before.

Things did not look good. I was facing a charge that could have resulted in life imprisonment had a jury been convinced that I intended to murder Mr Heseltine with a pack of dirty playing cards. I spent an uncomfortable few hours – what a waste of a night in a five-star hotel – until Vic Reeves's tour manager could be found to confirm that I was there to not star in his video. I was more than happy to return to Greenwich, though what little magic Mell Street had was extinguished.

My wild bachelor days and my link with Mell Street came to a sudden halt soon afterwards when I met the future Mrs Hardee: Jane. Apart, that is, from some early two-timing with the lovely twenty-four-year-old Lisa . . .

The first time Jane saw me I was naked behind Chris Lynam at Up the Creek. During his act, Chris sings 'It's a Wonderful World' semi-seriously and, while he's singing it, I walk on slowly, naked except for a pair of socks, a glass of beer and a cigarette. I sit on a chair behind him, smoking and drinking.

Jane had been living in Devon but when her marriage broke up she came to study humanities, or something similarly vague, at Thames Polytechnic (now the University of Greenwich). She and her sister had been going somewhere else that night, but something made them go into Up the Creek instead. After the show I went back to their house with them, had a bit of a bash and didn't get anywhere. But Jane and I got on well together from the start. I made one tragic mistake: I took her to the *Time Out* Awards for Comedy. The previous year at that event I'd announced my engagement to my flatmate Julia – but that had been a publicity stunt. It must have been in my mind though. This time, when Jane and I got back after the party and were in bed, I was in that mellow frame of mind that comes with semi-advanced drunkenness, and said: 'Ooaargh, we should get married.'

Instantly Jane got her three kids round the end of the bed, announced to them she was going to get married and was on the phone to her mother within the hour. I couldn't get out of it then but I never thought I'd ever actually get married.

Jane's recollection of events is slightly different. She insists that I proposed in the kitchen on bended knees. Memory plays funny tricks. Anyway, the *Time Out* Awards took place in September 1992 and we were married on April Fool's Day 1993. I wanted to have the ceremony on the *Cutty Sark*, the old sailing ship at Greenwich, and went to see the captain. It still has a captain and log book, even though it's in dry dock and can't go anywhere. Twenty-five years ago, or thereabouts, they logged a Man Overboard, when someone fell off and broke his leg.

The captain kindly agreed to our marriage being blessed on board but you couldn't get married in unusual places then. However, that captain left before we could make any arrangements and the new one would have none of it. He said I didn't have enough nautical tradition, which I thought was a bit of a cheek: my dad had pulled the *Cutty Sark* into her dry dock in the first place. I felt a little bitter about that.

We got married on a Thursday. The Bar de Musée in Blackheath had a 'singles night' on Wednesdays, which encouraged me to make what turned out to be another tragic mistake. I had my

182

stag night in the traditional way on the evening before the wedding. The only female who came was Julia, the previous year's 'fiancée', but Annie the German was staying at my house. She's about six foot five, looks like a bloke – imagine a cross between Marlene Dietrich and wrestler Mick McManus – and had come over especially for the wedding. She was my sister Clare's penfriend when they were kids and as a fifteen-year-old visitor to London she was drinking pints of Guinness, bottles of whisky, and smoking Players full-strength fags. She's larger than life in every way. Once she walked into my room, when I was in bed, and said: 'You vill sleep mit me. Now!' and jumped on top of me. She was only fifteen to my twenty-five. So I did – well, I *had* to. I was acting under orders. That went on for a couple of weeks until she went back to Germany.

Clare had kept in touch with Annie, but I didn't see her again until she came over for the wedding when it turned out she'd fancied me all these years. After I got home, drunk, from the stag night party she tried to get into bed with me. But I kicked her out. I was too drunk and, anyway, it wouldn't really have been on to do it the night before my wedding.

I'm not the best person to describe the day itself – I can't remember much of it. In the morning Annie the German gave me a bottle of rum, which turned out to be ten times the proof of the normal stuff. I'd only had a couple but I was soon staggering around in the suit I'd borrowed for the occasion from Jonathan Ross. When I got to the register office at Woolwich Town Hall, I couldn't even say my name. My mum and sister were laughing like drains but Jane's mum stormed out shouting, 'This isn't a wedding! It's a farce!' Somehow I've won her round since then.

After the register office, I went home and had four hours to recover before the church blessing ceremony at five o'clock – or so I thought. But Annie the German gave me another rum and spiked it with a hallucinogenic drug. I suppose she thought she was doing me a favour.

183

The 'blessing' was conducted at St Alfege Church in Greenwich, designed by Hawksmoor who was a mate of Christopher Wren. There are only five of his churches in London. Gavin, the local vicar, presided over a church full of guests. I think he was glad of the publicity for his church. I was kitted out at the shop where Julia works, Emporium, with tails and a top hat and all that game, though I didn't wear the hat except for the photos. It didn't look right on me. Someone had painted HELP! on the soles of my shoes – which I didn't know about – so that when I knelt down the congregation sniggered. I felt a bit faint half-way through, so I had to go and sit down. Martin Soan, my best man, took my place and it must have looked as if *he* was marrying Jane.

Arthur Smith did the Bible reading. I'd told him he could read anything he liked, provided it was from the Bible. The passage he chose was from Psalm 75:

> We give thanks to thee, O God, we give thanks.
> We call on thy name and recount thy wondrous deeds
> At the set time which I appoint I will judge with
>   equity
> When the Earth totters and all its inhabitants
> It is I who keep steady its pillars
> I say to the boastful
> Do not boast
> And to the wicked
> Do not lift up your *horn* [Arthur delivered this word
>   with heavy emphasis]
> Do not lift up your *horn*
> Do not lift up your *horn* on *high*
> Or speak with insolent neck
> For not from the East nor from the West
> And not from the Wilderness comes lifting up
> But it is God who executes judgement

Putting down one and lifting up another
For in the hand of the Lord there is a cup
With foaming wine well-mixed
And He will pour a draught from it
And all the wicked of the Earth shall drain it
Down to the dregs
But I will rejoice forever
I will sing praises to the God of Jacob
All the *horns* of the wicked he will *cut off*
But the *horns* of the righteous shall be *exalted*

I still wasn't feeling too well at the end of the service. When I came out of the church I'm told there was a photographer, but I went to this little vestibule toilet and apparently spent a quarter of an hour in there coughing. When I finally came out we all went to Up the Creek for the reception. In the car on the way, my sister set fire to her red taffeta dress. She'd been having a quick fag.

I had booked several acts to perform at the reception: a Russian balalaika band, led by Madelaine Wood's mother, Moth, a skiffle band called Please Yourself and my adolescent heroes Geno Washington and the Ram Jam Band. Eddie Shit, a little-known artist, was also on the bill: he sings well-known songs but substitutes 'shit' for odd innocuous words. It's one of the funniest acts I've ever seen. He was the drummer in The Macc Lads and, as Eddie Shit, he was also their support act on a tour when the other members of The Macc Lads didn't know that he and their drummer were the same person. As Eddie, he performed in a leotard and a circus-style moustache and they never saw through his disguise. He never actually performed at my wedding reception. He turned up, demanded his fee from my new wife and shot back to Liverpool. You don't hear a lot of Eddie Shit these days, but he's out there somewhere.

One conspicuous absentee from the wedding frolics was Wizo who, a couple of weeks before, had decided to return to Australia. About a year before, he had gone there for the first time in a state of collapse, after a harrowing Edinburgh Fringe where his divorce papers came through. He went full-tilt into exaggerating and had a series of disastrous relationships. He was in Australia for about three months, then came back to Britain and stayed with me. He said he'd met this glamorous model, Megan – pronounced *Meegan* in Australian – and got out some photos.

A few months later he said, 'Megan's coming over on holiday for two or three weeks. Can she stay in my room?'

'Yes,' I said, not wanting to refuse an old mate. Up the Creek was doing well and I had a Jaguar XJ6. Wizo also asked if he could borrow the car to pick her up from the airport. I don't like lending Wizo my cars because it always ends badly, but I said OK.

I didn't see much of Megan and Wizo to start with because all they did was have sex. This was a terrible thing because I thought the upstairs floor was going to give way. Gradually, though, they calmed down a bit and I discovered from Megan that Wizo had told her that the Jaguar and my house were his. He had told her not to take any notice of the mad old boy with the spectacles who lived downstairs so she thought I was taking advantage of Wizo, living in his house for free and using his phone a lot. He had also told her he owned Up the Creek but had neglected to mention that he had been married: he had referred to his ex-wife as his sister and had ignored the existence of his grandchildren. He had actually informed her that he'd never been married – and Megan must have thought she was on to a good thing with an unattached club owner who had a house in London and a Jaguar XJ6. Meanwhile, I had thought she was staying for three weeks but about six months passed.

In the end, I had to tell her the truth, that he didn't own the club. 'But,' she said, 'he must get a *bit* of a percentage.'

'Well, no,' I said. 'He doesn't.'

She got her own back. She told Wizo she had crabs.

After that, there were lots of rows and Wizo started telling everyone he hated her and was trying to get rid of her. However, when she had gone back to Australia, he sold me his computer and used the proceeds to join Megan in Adelaide, just a couple of weeks before my wedding. Silly bugger.

CHAPTER 13

MAINSTREAM, ALTERNATIVE, WEIRD

I found out in Edinburgh one year that I could sing opera. I had gone up to the Fringe with comedian Boothby Graffoe and had to wake him one morning at eight-thirty so he could go and do some TV thing. Although I'm in showbiz and people in showbiz generally get up late, I can get up in the morning because I've got kids. I'm used to it. That morning, I heard Pavarotti on the radio and woke Boothby by singing opera at him.

Boothby is from Lincolnshire. It's not his real name: he used to live near a village called Boothby Graffoe and remembered it when he was looking for a stage name. I first saw him when he was a mainstream comic. He had just stopped doing the Butlin's circuit and he and I were on a Granada TV pilot called *Stand Up*. He was still using straight mainstream material, though Joan Collins jokes rather than mother-in-law ones. Even then, though, he had this hippie-ish appearance: he did his act in a duffel coat. I didn't think I would get on with him, because he was such a mainstream comic.

I bumped into him again when I was running the Tunnel, took him up to the Edinburgh Fringe a couple of times and discovered that he's a good bloke. He was living in Leicester then, and I had just started going out with Jane, who had a Jack Russell called Roly – because it would look at you and then roll over. Roly was going blind when I took him to see Boothby. I'd never been to Boothby's house before and he had never met Roly.

Boothby and his wife lived in a bungalow, which didn't look like his taste at all: it was the sort of house an old person would live in. I looked through the window and saw Boothby out the back. I scribbled a little note and stuck it in Roly's collar. It read:

190

MY NAME IS ROLY
PLEASE LOOK AFTER ME

I tied him to the door then knocked and ran round the side of the house. When Boothby and his wife saw Roly and read the note, they agreed straightaway to keep him, which endeared Boothby to me.

He is one of those performers who just has 'It'. If you analyse his material, it isn't that good, but it's the way he delivers it – the casual approach. He can stand up and talk for half an hour on seemingly nothing and you laugh and have a great time. To move from mainstream to alternative he cut out a few of the Joan Collins jokes.

The rougher the audience the better Boothby likes it because then he has something to bounce off. There are limits, though: he was attacked by some nutcase at the 1994 Glastonbury Festival. Boothby hid behind a speaker but sensibly left the microphone switched on: 'There's someone here attacking me . . . Hello out there . . . He's coming to get me . . .'

Two or three years before that, I had been attacked at Glastonbury by a man called Bone, part of the anarchist group Class War. He was going on about how rich we all were – I must have been wearing a suit. He had a daughter called Jenny, who was a brilliant sixteen-year-old comic, the female equivalent of Gerry Sadowitz. I saw her do five or six gigs and never heard of her again. She must have given up, which is a great pity.

Some great comedians have given up when they might have gone on to greater things. Others have gone on to gain that success. Vic Reeves was one of the latter group. He should have given up.

Vic's a clever man. He used to perform in South East London

at the Goldsmiths' Tavern, next to Goldsmiths' College in New Cross. He called his stage show *Vic Reeves' Big Night Out* and did it with a local alcoholic called Alan King, who was the brains behind it but a less talented performer. Alan used to tell old Tommy Cooper jokes badly while he was ironing. Because the show's title included Vic Reeves's name, it was he who attracted the cult following. He used to spin a fan round and the audience all knew his catchphrases like 'Give it a spin!' and 'What's on the end of the stick, Vic?' Now and again, though, he'd come into the alternative cabaret circuit and he did the Open Spot a few times at the Tunnel. Most times he died.

After Alan King left him, Vic teamed up with Bob Mortimer and I got them a booking at Bracknell Arts Centre. It was an easy place to play, with about ninety in the audience in a little cellar. After Reeves and Mortimer played there, however, people signed a petition, saying they never wanted to see Vic Reeves or Bob Mortimer in the building ever again. The whole audience. A year later, the manager rang me to offer eight thousand pounds for them to perform in the big theatre next door.

When the Goldsmiths' Tavern got too small for him, Vic moved his show down the road to the Albany Empire. Michael Grade of Channel 4 was in the audience one night, which is how Vic got his first TV series. Success hasn't changed him: he was arrogant before he was successful. I get on OK with him, but he's not an easy man: the surreal nature of the show is a good indication of what he is like. You can have a conversation with him that's straight out of his show: 'I saw two cabbages walking down the road . . .' It's a bit like a schoolboy joke where only he and his mates are in on it. I didn't understand his show or think it was funny when I first saw it but, if you're told something's funny long enough, it becomes funny. Now I do find Reeves and Mortimer funny, if not hilarious, and certainly funnier than most mainstream comedy.

I think Michael Barrymore, a South East London boy from Bermondsey, is the best of the current mainstream comics. I saw him years ago when his act involved standing on his head doing impersonations of an Australian John Cleese. Early in his career, he was heavily backed by the *Daily Mirror*. They ran a series of pieces at yearly intervals on an unknown comic, Barrymore, reporting on his progress. I think that helped him along. He is extremely good at what he does, especially talking to ordinary people. He has just the right tone of cynicism but, like me, he also likes naff end-of-the-pier acts. He's encouraging yet, at the same time, rather tongue-in-cheek.

Whenever I'm asked who I think is the most talented alternative comedian who never made it as big as he should have, I always say Gerry Sadowitz, because he is a genuinely gifted magician-comedian. Recently I read Alexei Sayle quoted as saying he thought Gerry was the only current comic genius. But I don't think any of the alternative comedy circuit comedians have really made it. None are commanding the Michael Barrymore/Bruce Forsyth/Cilla Black level of income. Comics like Reeves and Mortimer are about five rungs down that ladder, still to an extent fringe comedians. Perhaps Lee Evans has done best: in his feature film, *Funny Bones*, he had equal billing with Jerry Lewis.

Lee Evans started as a mainstream comic, doing the Butlin's circuit before he linked up with alternative acts – probably because he was young. He is often compared to Norman Wisdom and there are similarities: both were boxers, both became fitness fanatics and they're both 'physical' comedians.

There are three mains types of comedy: mainstream – your bow-tie and frilly-shirt Jim Davidson show; alternative – which has an intellectual or even art content; and just plain weird. Some alternative acts latch on to the public consciousness and gain some mainstream success by adapting slightly but the nature of alternative comedy means it attracts a limited audience. The mainstream audience consists of people who watch BBC1 at eight-thirty on a weekday evening. Ben Elton and Rowan Atkinson have drifted across from alternative into mainstream and so have French and Saunders, who started off in the Comic Strip.

Charlie Chuck is a weird act, who should, theoretically, never make it. But if he goes the Freddie Starr route and tones down his act – which he has already started to do, since his appearances as Uncle Peter on *The Smell of Reeves and Mortimer* – he might. Weird is funny, but the general public aren't usually ready for it. About the nearest you can get to a weird mainstream act is either Freddie Starr or Spike Milligan.

Some acts, of course, are just too weird ever to make it. Like Ian Hinchcliffe, for example. I first heard about him long ago, even before I started with the Greatest Show on Legs. Someone once asked, 'Do you want to see this fellow called Ian Hinchcliffe who eats glass?' I didn't go, but years later, when he must have been in his fifties I saw him in various pub shows. He was, he said, a performance artist, and in one part of his act he would 'disembowel' himself. He would strap a bag under his jacket from which he would pull bits of liver and other offal as though it was coming from his stomach, then toss it into the audience. One show I saw was in an East End pub with a particularly rough landlord. The liver flew right over the audience's heads, hit the landlord and knocked off the optics behind the bar. The landlord came over to beat him up and Ian Hinchcliffe jumped out of the first-floor window. He landed on the landlord's car, putting a big dent in the bonnet. He wasn't asked back to that pub. At another gig in Birmingham, someone got up half-way through and left. Ian Hinchcliffe stopped the show and followed him home. Quite what the rest of the audience felt, I don't know. Audiences vary, of course.

In 1994, the Greatest Show on Legs went to the Melbourne Comedy Festival. We appeared on the long-running Australian TV show

Hey! Hey! It's Saturday! and the Balloon Dance fielded more complaints than anything else they'd ever screened. You never saw anything except our bums but viewers said it was tasteless.

While we were over there we met up with Wizo. He had been working at the Adelaide Festival but turned up in Melbourne. He had just broken up with Megan and was now apparently with some actress but was phoning Megan every ten minutes. In Australia his exaggerations aren't normally exposed very easily. Or they weren't until we arrived. A couple of the Melbourne acts told me they'd met a mate of mine called Wizo who had been in the British commandos. I knew he hadn't even been in the British Boy Scouts.

The audiences at the Melbourne Comedy Festival were expecting something different from us than what they got. They knew we did 'naked dancing', so our venues were filled largely with middle-aged, blue-rinsed women thinking they were going to see the Chippendales. It happens quite often that a good act gets the wrong audience, and it wasn't until the end of our run that we started getting the real comedy crowd.

The rock star Sting once invited Tommy Cooper to support the Police at the Milton Keynes Bowl. About 40,000 rock fans were waiting for Sting in this vast auditorium, many of them a good distance from the stage. To appreciate Tommy Cooper you had to see him close up and in this location he flopped. The fans were shouting, 'Come on, Sting! We want Sting!' and eventually beermats and other unidentified objects were flying at him. Ever the pro, Tommy Cooper ploughed on to the end. As he came off he passed Sting walking on, looked at him and said, 'Follow that!'

I once did a gig at a college for the disabled somewhere in the Midlands. I was on with Harry Hill, who did his normal routine, which included, 'You know what it's like when you're travelling on the tube . . . You know what it's like . . .' which of course, his audience didn't, because they were restricted to wheelchairs. He went off to muted applause . . . well, not even that because most of them couldn't applaud. I had watched this and thought, Well, you gotta give the audience what they want, so I went out and said, 'You know what it's like when you're running in the Marathon . . .' and played the mouth-organ for fifteen minutes. They liked that.

Jenny Eclair is another good act who has been stuck with the wrong audience. In the early 1980s, she was on at the Elephant Fair in Cornwall. An act called the Vicious Boys who, at the time, were popular as Children's TV presenters, were booked so there were crowds of fourteen-year-olds, as well as a few hippies and leather-clad Hell's Angels. I was compèring. When the Vicious Boys didn't arrive the organisers decided to put Jenny on instead at eleven o'clock in the morning. She came out in an evening dress and her opening line was, 'You know what it's like when you've been invited to a dinner-party . . .' They didn't like her.

Sometimes small audiences are better. Recently, I was in bed with Jane and leant back to read the paper. It's a brass bed and I got my head stuck between two stanchions. Jane shrieked with laughter for about fifteen minutes. We tried everything to get my head out and finally Vaseline did the trick. Jane plastered my head with it and it popped out. That day my audience of one gave me a better reaction than I've sometimes had performing to thousands.

Recently Jane and I were in Amsterdam where we went to see a live sex show, as you do when you're in Amsterdam – you have to, really. There was a building with a big front and lots of colour pictures of sexual goings-on and a man standing outside. I said, 'How much?'

It was equivalent to about thirty pounds each. I handed over the money and then we followed the man a mile across Amsterdam to where the show was happening. When we got there, I discovered that had we paid at the door we'd have got in for half what we had already handed over. We went into an old church with pews

still in it and sat right at the back, being shy, retiring types.
Half-way through I went to the toilet, as did several others – I
don't know what *they* were doing in there but I went in for a piss.
As I came out, I passed the next performer, a big-bosomed black
woman – rather like comedienne Brenda Gilhooley but in negative.
The show had reached the audience participation spot. I congratu-
lated myself on having sat at the back, but the big black woman
went right round the whole audience and picked me out. Jane
made me go up on stage.

The woman danced about a bit and I had to copy her move-
ments – she was probably the only black woman ever without a
sense of rhythm. Then she told me to sit down, which I did,
whereupon she sat down too, opened her legs and stuck a banana
up herself. She pointed at me, then at the banana. I got the message. I had to eat it where it was. Well, as you may have realised
by now, I'm game for anything once. I bent down to have a go –
and the banana shot out and hit me in the face.

Jane, bless her, tried to get me a booking for the next night's
show.

The most bizarre live sex show I ever saw was in Hamburg.
The Greatest Show on Legs were performing at the same place the
Beatles used to play: it had been converted into a TV studio. One
night we had gone on a sex tour and saw this sign:

PEEP SHOW – 2 MARKS

outside a semi-circular building with several doors each of which
had a money-slot. Steve Bowditch, Martin Soan and I selected a
door each, pushed in the coins and went in. Once inside, we found
ourselves standing next to each other, rather than in individual

cubicles, which is usually what happens in a peep show. But no. We were standing in the open, beside a woman on a bed that was moving round in a circle. She could see us, of course, just as well as we could see her.

She took a shine to Steve and struck up a conversation with him. 'You nice English boy,' and she told him she'd see him afterwards if he went to the man at the door and gave him some money. Steve always says the wrong thing. She was Brazilian but as she lay on the rotating bed with her legs wide open she said she came from America at which Steve asked, 'Grand Canyon?' She didn't laugh.

People go to shows for all sorts of reasons. Johnny 'Edge' Edgecombe sometimes comes to Up the Creek, but mainly for the disco music at the end of the evening. He goes to jazz clubs normally and, in fact, he's a jazz promoter. In 1963 he was Christine Keeler's pimp and fired the gun at her door, which precipitated the court case in which John Profumo, the Minister for War, was named as her lover. Johnny has written his own book now, because when the film *Scandal* came out he didn't like the way he was portrayed. For a start, they made him a Jamaican and he's from one of the other Caribbean islands.

CHAPTER 14

THERE WERE THESE TWO
PARAMEDICS . . .

Nineteen ninety-five was the twenty-fifth anniversary of the Glastonbury Festival and the year I had billed as my last Edinburgh Festival show. Neither was altogether true.

It *was* twenty-five years since the first Glastonbury Festival although in a few of those years it hadn't taken place, and I haven't ruled out the possibility of appearing occasionally at the Fringe, though probably not every year from now on.

As usual, I was compèring in the comedy tent at Glastonbury. The last act was a fellow called UltraVision who was basically a juggler. He used Dayglo luminous paint on his props so, if you were watching in the dark and you'd had a bit of dope, it must have looked quite good. I thought it was bollocks and I was thinking along those lines in the dressing room at the back where he kept all his paint. When the comedian Sean Lock walked by I said, 'Here, Sean, do us a favour. Can you paint my knob?'

He did – Dayglo yellow with red testicles. He decorated my nipples with little red circles and my belly-button with a yellow one. When UltraVision finished his act, I went on and said, 'Thank you very much, ladies and gentlemen. That was UltraVision. Twenty-five years of Glastonbury. My tribute . . .' Someone turned out the lights and put on a Bon Jovi record. I took off my clothes and I was away. I threw one of his clubs around, threw some of his Dayglo confetti up in the air, started having a wank and walked off. That night, I dreamt I had some sort of sex with Mrs Hardee after which we went off to one of those rave tents with ultraviolet lights. For some reason, she was going around looking like Al Jolson.

The Dayglo testicles proved a useful addition to my act in Edinburgh. It was the climax of my show, which lost four thousand pounds: the first time I had ever lost money on the Fringe.

Nineteen ninety-five, in fact, was a year of near death and destruction all round. The *Observer* had sent a young man called Sam Taylor to review the comedy on the Fringe. He knew nothing about the comedians or the history of it but planned to do the normal press thing of going along to the shows for which the big agents had sent press releases. Jane's brother-in-law is a photographer for the *Observer* and I was introduced to Sam Taylor. I invited him to review my show. 'Do you know anything about Edinburgh?' he asked, unaware that I was the self-styled King of the Fringe.

I didn't get on with him very well but he did turn up for my show – three days before the last night. As the *Observer* publishes on a Sunday, his piece wouldn't come out until after our show had finished its run. He hadn't seen the show before so I told him I did a bit of fake karate in which I got a volunteer to hold a bit of wood. He offered to do it. When the moment came, I said, 'Ladies and gentlemen, I used to do a bit of karate and I'd like a volunteer from the audience to hold this plank.' Sam Taylor came on stage and picked it up. I did the karate-style moves, then ran towards him and kneed him in the bollocks. He fell down and crawled off the stage.

I went up to the microphone. 'Sorry,' I said, 'I haven't done that for a long time.'

He got up the stairs and as far as the door where someone asked, 'Did you enjoy the show?'

'No,' he said.

'Are you going to give Malcolm a good review?'

'No,' he said. And, sure enough, he didn't: he described me as a balding, myopic lunatic.

I wasn't that myopic when I kneed him in the bollocks, though.

Last year, 1995, I was performing with Ricky Grover and the Bastard Son of Tommy Cooper. I'm not Ricky's agent but I help him a bit. I advised him to sign with the Avalon agency for a year, but they are now signing everyone up for five, which sounds rather like a sentence to me.

The Edinburgh Fringe is now working on the Supermarket Theory: big agents, like Avalon and Off the Kerb, take fifteen or twenty shows like a comedy conveyor belt. I used to go with one or two – like the little corner shop – and supply quality but I didn't necessarily get many customers.

Ricky Grover is a bit like a male Jo Brand. When she started performing as the Sea Monster, nearly all her material was about being fat. She is still accused of that although little of what she does now relates to excess flesh. A lot of Ricky Grover's material does, though. He's an ex-boxer in his mid-thirties, who was illiterate until three or four years ago. He has been a hairdresser and a criminal, a member of an East End gang in East Ham. On one robbery, he and his mates had been watching a bloke in a shoe shop. They were going to nick his takings – around fifteen grand – when he tried to put it in a night safe and followed him for three weeks. He kept the money in a pouch and Ricky's job was to go up to him – because Ricky looks quite threatening – and say, 'Look, give us the money, behave yourself and you won't get hurt.' He did this, grabbed the pouch, leapt in the car and off they drove.

After each robbery, they went to the home of the mum of one of the gang members for a cup of tea. They went there with the pouch, sat down and opened it. Inside were four ham sandwiches. The gang leader didn't bat an eyelid. He just said, 'One for you . . . One for me . . . One for you . . . One for you . . .'

Ricky went on a course eventually to learn how to read. He wanted to be an actor and wrote a play about boxing, *Punch*, part of which he performed at the Fringe. It was very powerful and the whole audience was quiet. It was filmed recently by a Swedish TV company. He became a comedian because when he first performed this play to his boxing chums it was so full of pathos and so many tears were shed that at the end he decided to tell a few jokes to lighten the atmosphere.

202

After his appearance at the Fringe he told me it hadn't been his sort of audience. He prefers to play the more mainstream Circus Tavern in Purfleet, Essex, near the M25. He says he likes 'thick' people like himself (his description, not mine). He goes down particularly well in Southend. The Edinburgh audience sat and stared at him and he almost lost his confidence. You do, if you haven't been in the game long and people don't react.

Most people just sat and stared at the Bastard Son of Tommy Cooper too. His real name is Sebastian. His father is Sicilian and his mother is English but he is small and wiry and speaks with a Welsh accent, because he was brought up in Swansea. His act is not for the squeamish. A couple walked out because they said they felt sick. He's a sword-swallower now, but he originally trained as a musician at Dartington College. It takes about a year to have your gullet open up enough to poke a sword down it and you have to practise every day.

When I took him to the Edinburgh Fringe, the Bastard Son of Tommy Cooper was getting fed up with his girlfriend. Half-way through the Fringe, he phoned her up to say it was all over. We asked how the conversation went and he said, 'She took it quite well.'

This was at about two o'clock. By five, she was on the phone again and he was looking sheepish. When he hung up he put on the answerphone in case she rang again.

We were all in the kitchen when the phone went and heard her slightly Welsh voice on the machine: 'I'm going to tell the whole world what this Bastard's like, what he's done to me.' We all stood in the kitchen listening, Ricky Grover, me, Steve Bowditch and the Bastard, who was looking sheepish again. 'Before he left for Edinburgh,' her voice continued, 'he smashed up the kitchen, broke the living-room window and kicked me in the cunt.' Then she slammed down the receiver.

Ricky said, 'What was wrong with that? That's what I do to

my wife if she don't get me breakfast on time. I thought I was going to hear something good like you were a paedophile!'

Three days later, I was on stage rounding off our show. I got to the words, '. . . and let's have a big round of applause for the Bastard Son of Tommy Cooper,' when I heard a cat miaow. This was a bit strange. I mentioned the Bastard again and once again the cat miaowed. I couldn't see where the sound was coming from, but we ended the show with no problems.

At the Fringe, you have to pack up fast to let the next performers prepare for their show. When the lights went up, there stood the Bastard's girlfriend Louise, in front of the stage, clutching a rather worried cat, yelling, 'He's a bastard!'

A woman from Latvia was in the audience and wanted to take photos of me, Ricky and the Bastard to show her friends back home. She was trying to get us into a group for the picture with her and her boyfriend while we were trying to clear up and get out at the same time as this argument started between the Bastard and his girlfriend.

I said, 'Nice cat, Louise.'

'Yes,' she said. 'And he's got very sharp claws.' With that, she threw the cat at the Bastard. It flew through the air, scratching my shoulder as it screeched towards him.

'Well,' I said, 'you'd better sort this out outside,' and shovelled Louise, the Bastard and the cat into the street. We tried to get on with packing up, but the Latvian woman was still screaming about the photos. Thank God my friend Maurice Gibb, the fireman, had been in the audience. He looks a bit like the Bastard Son of Tommy Cooper – or, at least, he was the nearest I could get. I persuaded him to pose with Ricky and me and the Latvian woman didn't notice the difference.

That night, Louise and her cat moved into our Edinburgh flat. Things were tense – Louise wasn't speaking to any of us and the cat was neurotic. Which, I suppose, was not surprising. After

about four or five days of this, I had to tell the Bastard that Ricky
was upset: he'd said hello to Louise that morning and she'd ignored
him.

When Louise got in she went mad, ranting on and on about
the Bastard being a bastard and calling Ricky Grover a pimp and
Jane a 'man-pleaser'. Jane was quite flattered.

Then Ricky went berserk at being called a pimp, because he
said he'd only ever worked in a brothel and he'd never been a
pimp and his little kid was in the flat with us. It was two in the
morning and the Bastard was crying. Jane took control: she told
the Bastard and Louise they'd have to leave the next morning or,
if they kept at it, they'd have to leave immediately. Louise clattered
out, shouting, 'I'm going to go to the papers!'

'I wish you would,' I said. 'We could do with the publicity.'

After she'd left, the Bastard said, still a bit tearful, 'Can you
feed the cat for Louise?'

Feed the cat? We'd have fed a lion to get rid of Louise.

She went back to London and, when last heard of, she had
moved to a caravan in Devon and was having therapy.

The next night we went to a Latin-American club for a bit of
relaxation. I left alone at about two o'clock after someone at the
club gave me three Ecstasy tablets. When I got back to our flat I
took one; I had had it before, but a long time ago at the Glastonbury Festival. It had been all right there, out in the fields, but,
this time, the effect was completely different.

Soon after I'd swallowed it Jane arrived back at our flat with
some lunatic bloke who'd heard I had the Ecstasy. I sold him a
tab and made a profit. He and Jane were going off to a rave and
I said, 'I'll come!' but I was in my dressing gown and by the time
I was ready they'd buggered off and I couldn't remember where
to go. So I took another half tab of Ecstasy.

A few minutes later, my heart started to beat faster and faster.
I wandered about the flat, my heart thumping madly, until

I thought, 'That's it! I'm going to die!' and lay down on the bed.

Jane got back at about six-thirty in the morning and I said, 'I'm going to die. I'm going to have a heart-attack.'

She tried to be calm and said, 'You're not. Just breathe properly.'

'I am!' I said. 'I'm going to have a heart-attack! Definitely!'

My heart was pounding and I was getting more and more paranoid. I told Jane she had to phone an ambulance, which, eventually, she did.

'They're on their way, aren't they?' I asked. 'I'm going to die!'

Panic is the word. Panic. According to Jane, I was lying on the bed with my pants on fiddling with my genitals, but I don't remember that. I was panicking about the ambulance not arriving.

After what seemed like a lifetime the doorbell rang. 'Thank God!' I said. 'They're here!'

It was the postman.

When two paramedics appeared in green gear my pulse rate was thirty beats over what it should have been, which isn't bad. They told me they'd had people with 150 over who had lived, but they had to take me to hospital just in case. They brought a chair with wheels on it to take me down the stairs, sat me in it, put a blanket over me and tied me in. I looked like Hannibal Lector from *Silence of the Lambs*. It was the most frightening thing I've ever experienced.

I told them I'd taken a tab and a half of Ecstasy – they don't have to report it to the police – and that I'd had a fair amount to drink. I found out later it was the drink that had caused the problem.

In the ambulance, one of them asked Jane how old I was. When she told him, he said, 'He should be old enough to know better.' Then he asked, 'Is he his normal colour?'

'He is now,' she said, 'but he looked a bit grey earlier on.'

I pulled down my oxygen mask at that and chipped in, 'But I've got luminous testicles!'

The paramedics looked at each other and I looked at them, then pulled down my trousers to display my Dayglo glory. It was all part of the show but they thought I was mad.

Once at the hospital, it was like having an MOT. They did all the tests and said I was remarkable for a man of my age. Later on I felt fine. We did a good show that night and I went out again until about four a.m.

Ricky Grover had trouble too. On his first night, the show went well and, afterwards, we went with a lot of other performers to the Gilded Balloon, where there's a show called *Late 'n' Live* but all you do is hang around in the bar and talk bollocks.

An excellent performer called Ian Cognito was there too, very drunk, as is his wont. When he's drunk, he gets aggressive. Part of his Italian upbringing, I think.

Ricky had worked with him before, so said hello to him, but Cognito grabbed him by the collar and said, 'You're a fat cunt!' Ricky doesn't mind that sort of thing – he's used to it – so Cognito continued, 'You're a fat cunt and you're not funny!'

Ricky stayed shtum, so Cognito added, 'And your wife's a fat cunt too!' which upset Ricky at last, because he's one of those traditional people.

'Did you mean that?' he asked.

'Yeah,' Cognito replied.

'Can you repeat it?' Ricky asked politely.

Cognito said, 'Your wife's a fat cunt.'

With one blow, Ricky knocked him out. Unconscious. Displaced his jaw. The lot. Ricky's a professional, so he knows exactly where to hit someone.

Standing three or four yards away was Jon Thoday, who runs the Avalon agency. I looked over at him and said, 'Have you got that £500 you owe me?' Funnily enough, the cheque arrived in the post about two days later.

While Ian Cognito was unconscious another well-known agent rushed over and told Ricky he shouldn't hit comedians and that he, the agent, could have people killed. This fellow's gone a bit funny. He behaves as if he's a villain but his father is a distinguished academic and he comes from a posh family. He likes to be laddish, though, and he's gone a step further now: he's got himself the black Crombie, the waistcoat, everything the well-dressed villain should have. A real villain I know saw him in the West End. The agent told him he was one of the Brindle Brothers. A bit of a feud was going on at the time, which included occasional shootings, in South East London. David Brindle was killed at the Bell in Walworth. His brother Tony was put under armed police protection but, some time later, when Tony came out of his house, he was shot too despite the police protection.

It was probably linked to the Frankie Fraser shooting: 'Mad Frankie' was shot in the head but survived. When I saw him in Edinburgh, doing his show, he said he was convinced he had been shot by undercover police who didn't want him to publish his autobiography. In his show, 'Mad Frankie' was talking about how he'd cut people up and so on. He was very cold and in comedy you have to have charm. You have to see the funny side of anything.

Anyway, back to Ian Cognito lying on the ground in Edinburgh, out cold. Once he came to, he was thrown out because Ricky was still in the club and the bouncers, who were half Ricky's size, decided to chuck out Ian. I arranged for Ricky and Ian Cognito to meet up the next day at the Assembly Rooms. Cognito admitted he had deserved what he got, with which most people seemed to agree.

I get on OK with him when he's sober. Before the Edinburgh incident I bought my current boat from him. He sold it to me because, after splitting up from his wife, he moved to Bath where

208

it would have been no use to him. I knew he wouldn't like it down there – and he doesn't – because, like me, he's a city boy.

I sailed that boat down the Thames flying the Jolly Roger and, as usual, I was stopped by the river police, who informed me that not only was it illegal to fly the Jolly Roger but I could be hanged for doing so. It's one of the three offences which still carry the ultimate penalty: treason, arson in a Royal Naval Dockyard and piracy, which includes flying the Jolly Roger. One of those quaint British laws administered by those quaint British police.

The man who lives over the road from me was on holiday in Turkey when these quaint British police broke into his house – they left fifteen sledge-hammer marks on his door. They suspected him of dealing drugs which, as far as I know, he doesn't, but at they didn't find anything except a police helmet they arrested him for possession of that. He'd bought it off a stall in Camden Market as a joke.

I'm happy when I'm out on my boat. The river is part of my family tradition, as you may remember, and I love a bit of tradition. Recently I took it from Greenwich to Runnymede for repair: the engine was firing on two instead of three cylinders, and the job was expected to take two days.

At Hampton Court bridge, I was passing a pub that fronts on to the river and heard the voice of comedian Nobby Shanks floating out of what I discovered was a comedy club called Screaming Blue Murder. I stopped, moored up for the night and went in. The manager seemed to know who I was, so I offered to do five minutes at the end. He accepted enthusiastically.

During the course of the evening I got a bit drunk but I went on stage anyway and did a few minutes of my normal stuff, which went down well. Then I decided to do a magic trick and asked for two volunteers from the audience. I got one to give me a fiver and the other a tenner, made them sign the notes and put them in an envelope. Then I said, 'Thank you very much. Goodnight,' and walked out of the pub, got in my boat and fucked off.

The manager, Pete Harris, demanded the money back when I saw him at the Edinburgh Fringe because he had had to give it back to the punters but he didn't get it: the incident was reported in *Time Out* and got him more publicity for his club.

A few weeks later, someone stole my boat's engine and I did a boat-engine benefit at Up the Creek. Everyone who had been on the boat performed for free to raise money for a new one. Then I had the boat towed back to Runnymede – a day's trip – and left it for the engine to be fitted. It's a cabin cruiser, which is only meant to travel at about 5 m.p.h. But I had decided to have a sixty-horse-power engine installed so it could go at about 30 m.p.h., which is fast for a boat like that.

When it was ready I took it out for a trip with Ricky Grover, Jane and her fifteen-year-old son William. The fellow who had installed the engine hadn't been able to fix the gear and speed control on the side of the boat because there wasn't a panel. He said, 'Just put it on your lap for the time being and, when you get back to Greenwich, put a panel on the side so you can fit the control on.'

At Runnymede, the boat-repair yard is on a little inlet which runs into the Thames. Down there the river is completely different from what it's like at Greenwich: at Runnymede, it's non-tidal and full of posh boats with posh people and that day they were sitting on the decks drinking tea in the sun. I turned on the engine and pushed the control forward. It went full throttle and we shot out, narrowly missing one or two canoeists who were already in a race but were now paddling as if they were in the Olympics.

The throttle cable had jammed on full. With great presence of mind I remembered not to turn right, which led towards the lock and the weir and went left. Ricky was standing at the stern and William was on the bow, prone, hanging on for dear life and screaming. The whole of the Runnymede river community seemed to be standing on their decks bellowing, 'Slow down!'

But I couldn't stop.

One man cried, 'My crockery!' As we tore past, I just had time to see him trying to catch all these delicate little china cups as the wash from my boat rocked his. Ricky didn't know what to do, so he just stood at the stern looking aggressive.

I went upriver for about a mile only to find another lock and weir. I still couldn't slow down, so turned round. Back in Runnymede, things had calmed down and the crockery man was putting his stuff back on the shelves – until I rocketed past his boat again. In the end, I found the key and switched off. I looked round at Ricky and said, 'It's just common sense, isn't it?' People in Runnymede are still talking about it.

I feel at peace on the river. And I'm happy living in Greenwich, running Up the Creek. If anything else comes along, that's fine too.

CHAPTER 15

EVEN FROM RELATIVES

I'm considering standing for Parliament again and think I have a better chance this time. Someone once called himself a Literal Democrat at a Euro-election and he didn't lose his deposit because a lot of people voted for him thinking he was the Liberal Democrat. He got loads of votes and nearly got in. The real Liberal candidate complained because he reckoned he would have got in if this rival hadn't 'stolen' his votes. I'm going to call my party Old Labour. I'll do whatever comes along.

I've got all the normal vices: smoking, drinking, gambling, womanising. I drink at weekends and sometimes on Wednesday nights but, by and large, I don't drink on weekdays and I don't drink during the day. I smoke between twenty and forty cigarettes a day, but I'm quite healthy, quite strong – maybe because of all that exercise in Borstal, detention centres and prison when I was younger.

I'd like to be thought of as a good bloke. Someone who won't let you down. I'm loyal. I'm unfaithful to women but the friends I've got I've had since school and I always like to keep in touch with people. Most people move on and go through different groups of friends but nearly everyone I meet I keep in some sort of contact with, even if it's not regular.

Last year, Dexie Doug Davies phoned me at Up the Creek, desperate. I was about to go on stage and I couldn't understand what he was saying. Something about how he had a girlfriend or a wife and she'd gone mad and run away with four or five kids and she was about to be put in a psychiatric hospital and he wanted to come up and see me. Normal for him. But he never appeared, so after a few months I reckoned he was either mad or dead or had sorted it out for himself.

Then he turned up at my annual birthday show. He was living down in Devon, hadn't worked for months, had fathered another couple of children. Nothing much had changed. He wanted to stay at my place but he's the type who, if he stays one night, ends up living with you for months. Jane said he was the most normal man she'd ever met.

I know all sorts of normal people. I admire Martin Potter, who was my partner at the Tunnel, best man at my register office wedding and handles the sound at Up the Creek. He's regular and calm, though he's secretive. I've known him for years. Not long ago, I saw Martin walking along the road with a kid of five or six. And it was *his* kid. He'd never mentioned it.

I have a brother, but I don't know him very well, because he's twenty years younger. I hardly saw him when he was a baby because I was in prison. When he started going to school, I was in my mid-twenties and selling ice-creams outside his school. He was quite proud of me then, because I was the Ice-cream Man. He sat his A Levels and passed them, then sat the Oxbridge exam and passed that but went to Manchester University instead. He wanted to do aeronautical engineering but a year into the course he decided to run a club. I sent him a list of performers and he got the showbiz bug. Then he found a partner and ran a comedy agency called Hardee Arts. That lasted three or four years – and was quite successful – until he split from his partner and moved to London, having signed a contract guaranteeing not to get involved in comedy for the next five years as long as the partner took on the debts of the business. Now he's got a job with Louis Parker at the Concord Agency, the Greatest Show on Legs' first agent. He's in the jazz-funk area of music and has been all over Japan.

But I'm happy where I am in South East London. I'm respectable now. I have trousers, a house and a wife.

While I was writing this book, I took part in an episode of a Radio 4 series called *Sentimental Journeys*. After the broadcast, the producer received a letter from a listener, which he passed on to me.

I was very interested in the last episode with Malcolm Hardee in which he talked about the 40th birthday party for Freddie Mercury. His explanation of what happened to the cake has helped to clear up a mystery for me.

At the time of this party, I was working as a chef in a Michelin-rated restaurant in Covent Garden, the Boulestin. The chefs at the Boulestin used to help out on occasion with the catering at Xenon, a nightclub in Piccadilly. We were doing the catering on the evening of Mr Mercury's birthday party.

After Freddie Mercury had posed for photos with a knife held over the pink Rolls cake it was removed to the kitchen. We were then told to cut and serve just small portions to the guests as the rest was going to be auctioned the next day for charity. After we had served the cake we moved it to the corridor, where it was cooler, and balanced it on the backs of two chairs.

It was some time later we found it gone, but assumed it had been removed for the auction. We didn't realize it had been stolen until the following Monday when the police turned up at the restaurant to ask questions to which we had no answers!

I was glad to hear it went to a good home.

Two final points. The cake was only decorated on one side as it was delivered to me at Xenon undecorated, twenty minutes before it was presented, and after Malcolm had been told he could not do his act with his balloons, two 'local' girls were found along with a lot of jelly and a plastic swimming pool!

Yours faithfully,
Simon Gibbs.

It's good to be remembered.

Two days before the publisher's deadline for this manuscript, the National Film Theatre in London ran *Another Night With the Bonzos*, an evening of films and reminiscences with surviving members of the Bonzo Dog Doo Dah Band. I thought about going, but didn't. It would have been nice to meet Neil Innes again, but I suppose he wouldn't have recognised me.

I think I'm popular with most people. But not everybody. Every year I send out Christmas cards. Last year's was based on a Renaissance painting in which the Virgin Mary is holding the baby Jesus. On my card, though, she had me in her arms with a pint of Guinness in my hand. It said:

MALCOLM HARDEE AND UP

THE CREEK

WISH YOU A MERRY CREEKMAS

AND A HAPPY FEW BEERS

I rang up my mum to get a few relatives' addresses and I sent one to my cousin Geoffrey, the one who had provided us with Boy Scout uniforms many years ago. On Christmas Eve I got a letter from him addressed to M. Hardee Esq., with my card enclosed. It said:

> Dear Malcolm,
> Your apology for a Christmas card is returned,
> although one is fearful of the consequences of

dispatching such unseemly material through the
Royal Mail. Whilst appreciating your probable aim
of sending Christmas greetings to members of your
family, neither my mother nor I appreciate
receiving blasphemous and disrespectful
communications at any time, even from relatives.
    Yours sincerely,
    Geoffrey E. Morriss.

As I said, it's good to be remembered.

INDEX

Lou, Great Uncle 11
Louise (plus the Bastard and a cat) 203–5
Lovell, Terry 96–7
Lovett, Bill 68–9
Luby, Chris 104, 124, 161–3, 166, 169–70
LWT 106, 109–10
Lynam, Chris 90, 102, 155, 160–1, 172

McCartney, Paul 24
The Mace Lads 185
McKenzie, Mr (asaulted office manager) 38–9
McNulty, John 94–5
Mad Mick (fork-lift truck driver) 122
The Mad Show 103–6, 124, 161–2
Madame Poulet and Her Singing Chicken 152
Manilow, Barry 145
Margaret, Princess 114
Marmalade 39
Maude, Nanny (grandmother) 5, 10
Maxted, Steve 39, 41
Mayall, Rik 100, 102, 108, 109, 111, 135
Megan (Wizo's Aussie model) 186–7, 195
Melbourne Comedy Festival 194–5
Mercury, Freddie, and his cake 114–15, 216

Merrick, Mazzie 78
Merton, Paul 135, 173
Methane, Mr (farteur) 117
Michael (leaf gluer) 84
Miles and Millner 169
Milligan, Norman 105
Milligan, Spike 40, 108, 137, 160, 194
minicab driving 84, 85, 86–7
Minns, Mr and Mrs (political incompatibles) 76
Mitre pub (Greenwich) 134–8, 154
Miwurdz (Hurst), Mark 152, 169–70
Modern Jazz Quartet 40
Mods and Rockers 39, 42, 43–4
Molony, John 164
Monahan, Rinty 4
Monstrous Regiment 118–19
Moran, Mr and Mrs (patient neighbours) 7–8
Morgan, Stuart 43
Morris, Geoffrey (cousin) 107–8, 217–18
Mortimer, Bob 192, 193
Moy, Mandy, 99, 128
Moy brothers 99

Nail, Jimmy 180
National Revue Company 117, 118
New Fundation 100–2
Newman, Delphi 128
Newman, Rob 88, 133
Newman, 'Stinks' 29–30
Niblett, Sally 84–5

Rogers, Terri 163–4, 166
Roly (blind roll-over dog) 190–1
Rosemary, Aunt 5, 48
Rosengard, Pete 103
Ross, Jonathan 183
Rowlan, John, Val and Simon
    137–8

Sadowitz, Gerry 145–9, 163, 167,
    193
St Dunstan's school 22–3
St Stephen's school 21–2, 23–4,
    26, 28–9
Sales, John 43
Saunders, Jennifer 194
Saward Baker advertising agency
    37, 38–9
Sayle, Alexei 103, 109, 110, 135,
    193
The Scotsman 151
Scott (Kiwi roadie) 96
Screaming Blue Murder club
    (London) 209–10
Screaming Lord (David) Sutch 76
Sedgehill Comprehensive 30–1, 32
Sensible Footwear 125
sex shows 134, 196–8
sexual hits (Malcolm's) 61, 78, 94,
    99, 117, 129, 179
    and misses 58, 65, 179, 183
Shanks, Nobby 209
Sherlock, Barry 3, 18–19, 22, 88
Sherlock, Pat 3
Sherrin, Ned 166
Shit, Eddie 185

Sid, Uncle 12, 75
Sinatra, Frank: birthday surprise
    144
Skinner, Frank 132–3
Skinner, Phil 100
Skint Video 125, 130, 131, 135,
    167
Sky TV 176
Small Faces 39
Smallest Theatre in the World 88,
    99, 109
Smith, Arthur (Brian) 117, 118,
    123, 135, 143, 151, 153–4,
    162, 184
Smith, Paul 21–2
Smith, PC Ron 74
Smith, Ronnie (sub-aqua pianist)
    104, 106
smoking wild rhubarb 60
Snakebite Award 124–5
Soan, Martin
    Babs Sutton's boyfriend 117
    Freddie Mercury's birthday
        cake 115
    Greatest Show on Legs 86–91,
        95, 99–102, 107–9, 121, 136,
        159–60
    Malcolm's sidekick 118, 130,
        184, 197–8
Squeeze 88, 129, 138, 177
stage advice 132–3
Starr, Freddie 194
Stax 39
Steele, Tommy 3
Steiner, Christian 99, 100

Variety, Mr, and his banjo 26–7
Vic (impractical mechanic) 84, 85
Vicious Boys 196

Walker, Johnnie 40
Walker, Peter 65
Waller, J.J. 104
Wandsworth prison 63–4
Ward, Don 103
Washington, Geno 39, 185
Watts, Pete 52, 53–5
Weiss, George 76
Westward Television 91
whales saved 125
Whiplash, Miss (famous neighbour) 3
Whitehouse, Mary 105, 110
Whitelaw, Billie 48–9
The Who 39
Wicked, Lily 149
Wide, Adam 117, 153–4
Willesden Empire 178

William (Jane's son) 210–11
Wilsford Manor, Wilts 10–12
Windsor, Barbara 48
Wisdom, Norman 3, 19, 193
Wiseman, Wizo
  partner in crime 18, 23, 51–5, 62–3, 65–7
  showbiz non-career 123, 131, 162, 166–7, 171–2, 176
  teenage father 50–1
  unlikely lifeguard 84
  up and doing down under 186–7, 195
Witchdoctor club (Catford) 39–41
Wonfor, Geoff 144
Wood, Deirdre 76
Wood, Madelaine, and family 74–6, 185
Wright, Jonty 129

Yates, Paula 144

Zap Club (Brighton) 158–9